Istanbul 50 Unsung Places

Lisa Morrow

Istanbul 50 Unsung Places
Copyright © Lisa Morrow 2023
ISBN 9798394863882

DEDICATION

First I'd like to thank my lovely husband Kim Hewett. He supports my writing in all sorts of ways, from listening to me endlessly debate which adjective is best to use, to cooking dinner and doing the washing up when it's really my turn. Most of all I appreciate his unerring faith in my abilities.

Then there's Jane Gündoğan, another Australian and author of fabulous chick lit set in Turkey and the best and only guide to Mersin, on the south east coast of the Mediterranean. She's a great friend and helped me stay focussed when I thought I couldn't write another word.

Finally, I'd like to say *Çok teşekkürler* to the hundreds of people I've spoken to in Istanbul over the years, while out and about researching, photographing, taking notes and looking for answers to my endless stream of questions. I've chatted with passengers on buses, security guards at tombs, cleaners in mosques, women in prayer rooms, waiters in restaurants, guides in museums, priests in churches and more people than I can possibly mention. All of them have readily given me their time and patiently answered my questions framed in less than perfect Turkish. In true Turkish style, they were generous with their knowledge and personal stories, teaching me things about Turkey and myself I never expected to learn.

Istanbul 50 Unsung Places is dedicated to you all.

Table of Contents

INTRODUCTION

Aziz Mahmud Hüdayi Mosque

In Istanbul minarets pierce the skyline, the call to prayer echoes off the clouds and the tantalising smell of food dances on the waves of the Bosphorus. It's no wonder this vibrant Turkish metropolis has long ignited the imagination of travellers, historians and writers alike. Early accounts by visitors such as Ogier Ghiselin de Busbecq, Lady Mary Wortley Montagu and Edmondo de Amicis recount scenes of daily life and palace machinations under the Ottomans. More recent books by Hilary Sumner-Boyd and John Freely provide useful guides full of detailed descriptions of the ancient remains of the city's past, making it easy to imagine life as it had once been. Then there's Orhan Pamuk whose stories and memoirs evoke the pathos and joy of living in a city where tradition and modernity mix, creating a seductively uneasy chaos. Despite their differences in time, genre and understanding, each author had the same aim. To capture and describe the city's essence for those who share their passion.

As I have come to know, pinning down exactly what it is that makes Istanbul so fascinating to so many people from varied backgrounds, cultures and religions is no easy task. There's a multitude of perspectives and even agreeing on what name to use is up for debate. Istanbul is the destination seen in airports but some still call it Byzantium, while for others it's forever Constantinople. Then there's older nicknames such as Asitane, a word that comes from the Persian. Asitane has two meanings, one referring to the theological and the other to the secular. The latter, meaning door or gateway, feeds into the popular trope of Istanbul as a city that straddles two continents.

Seen on a map Istanbul does stretch from Asia Minor across to Europe but using this geographical metaphor to describe the city is too simplistic. In reality there's no neat divide between east and west. Even when the Ottomans conquered Istanbul in 1453, the city was already home to a mixed population including Byzantine Greeks known as Rum, Turkic speaking Muslim converts originating from Central Asia, and Seljuks from Persia, to name a few. Not long after the conquest Jews arrived from Spain, settling on the shores of the Golden Horn where Yeni Camii, the New Mosque, now stands. Over the following centuries many more passed through the gates, fleeing in search of asylum or seeking better opportunities. Some stayed and made new homes in Istanbul while others, like the majority of the 200,000 White Russians who came to Istanbul in November 2018 escaping the Bolshevik Revolution moved on, leaving little behind.

Given this history, I prefer to envision Istanbul as Asitane, a gateway opening onto both Europe and the East simultaneously, through which thousands of people have passed. Over time however, a lot of the diversity has been buried, sometimes literally. When new cultures arrived many used Byzantine stones to manufacture their own infrastructures, developing new communities on top of and amongst existing ones. Not only did they partially or completely cover over multi-layered traces of past histories, they also displaced existing groups who called Istanbul home. In the 20th century numerous events occurred that further disrupted and disconnected ethnic minorities from their roots in both Istanbul and Turkey. Some were accidental and others intentional, resulting in people being made to leave the country or going into self-exile before it was forced upon them.

It's important to remember that Istanbul is more than the sum of the historical sites so admired by tourists. It's a living city in which the human landscape continues to evolve and change. All the hundreds and thousands of souls who did and do call Istanbul home have left their mark in some way, provided you know where to look. You can still see an Orthodox church side-by-side with a synagogue and a mosque, or watch Greek youth dive for the

3

Cross on Epiphany. The once predominantly Armenian neighbourhoods of Samatya and Kumkapı on the northern shores of the Sea of Marmara are now home to relative newcomers from Central Asia and the African Continent and in many neighbourhoods, Arabic is more often heard than Turkish.

I have a list of places to see in Istanbul and have spent more than ten years going to different neighbourhoods, visiting tombs, statues, art galleries, museums, mosques, churches, synagogues and other places of interest. I talk with worshippers, security guards, restaurant staff, street vendors, cleaners and council staff, ask questions, listen to stories and connect with people. I never get to the end of my list because as soon as I've written up my notes and satisfied my curiosity about one thing I've seen, I've added another two. Some I've read about or been told of by one of the many people I meet. Often I'll see something from a bus window or when I'm on my way home after a long day exploring that I hadn't noticed before. I'll take a photo or make a note of the name and location, to visit another time. Leisurely aimless ambles through small ordinary looking leafy streets on balmy summer mornings or bright sunny cold winter days often yield the best treasures.

I'm a very organised person but when it comes to Istanbul there's no rhyme or reason as to why I chose particular places to share with you. This is not a definitive guide because Istanbul is like a kaleidoscope made up of little windows from the past, viewed in the present. It reveals itself through one small glimpse at a time, each frame teeming with life, colour and sound. In *Istanbul 50 Unsung Places* you will discover the Istanbul that piques my interest, keeps my attention and has captured my heart. The places where I believe you'll come close to feeling the city's essence, ever elusive but always entrancing, even if just for a fleeting moment. The majority of them lie outside the more travelled tourist zones with their grand narratives because my Istanbul exists in the small details, where the everyday extraordinary of life in modern Istanbul resides. Let *Istanbul 50 Unsung Places* take you there.

Lisa Morrow
April 2023

TURKISH SPELLING AND PRONUNCIATION

Throughout this book Turkish spelling has been used for most Turkish names and for things that are specifically Turkish. Turkish words are pronounced phonetically and letters that do not occur in English or are pronounced differently are explained below.

Vowels are pronounced as follows
a as *a* in *father*
e as *e* in *met*
ı as *u* in *but*
ö as *oy* in *annoy*
ü as *e* in *new*

Consonants are generally pronounced as in English with the following exceptions.
c as *j* in *jam*
ç as *ch* in *choose*
g as in the hard *g* in *get*
ğ is called soft g and lengthens the preceding vowel sound
ş as *sh* in *sharp*

HOW TO USE THIS BOOK

Istanbul 50 Unsung Places is designed to use as a standalone self-guide, with history, little known facts, transport information, directions and handy tips located all together so when you arrive at your destination, all you have to do is soak up the atmosphere. It's aimed at people who want to breathe in their surroundings rather than always look at their phone for directions. The entries are listed in Turkish. This means if you get lost or aren't sure which direction to take, you can show people in shops or at transport stops where you want to go next. However the entries are listed in the index in English, allowing you to easily decide where you want to visit.

Outside of major tourist areas not so many people speak English or other languages but wherever you are Turks are generally very helpful. It's quite common for them to ask someone they know who does speak English to assist you or even call them on the phone for you to speak with them. Do note though, they will give you directions even if they aren't sure of the way. As a rule of thumb ask three people before heading off. It might be a less reliable method than using your phone but this way you get the chance to connect with Turkish people out and about doing everyday, ordinary things.

Wherever possible, I've included old fashioned practical information about public transport and where to walk once you step off a bus, ferry, tram or train. When I haven't done this it's because the directions are so complicated they'd need a page all to themselves. If you're like me, trying to remember when to turn left and then right, or was that right and then left, never works. In these cases, depending on your preference, check on the map before you go, screenshot the walk or if you have Wi-Fi, follow the route live once you're out on the road. Unless I explain otherwise, assume the return journeys are the reverse of the way you came.

In some instances I've suggested catching a taxi, particularly when the walk is up a steep hill. Istanbul is known as the city of seven hills but in reality there are many more. Getting around solely using public transport and on foot requires a good level of fitness and mobility. Street surfaces are often uneven, sidewalks very crowded and some hills suitable for Olympic slalom competitions. Do bear in mind your own physical abilities and comfort levels when planning explorations based on the entries in this book.

All the details concerning opening times were correct at the time of publication. The timing of public holidays based on the Islamic calendar such as Ramazan and Kurban Bayramı changes every year. For information about these and all the other national holidays see the latest guide to Turkish National Public Holidays on my website Inside Out In Istanbul. You'll find the post under Practical Information in the Categories drop down on the right-hand side of the page.

PUBLIC TRANSPORT IN ISTANBUL

Şehirhat ferry docked at Beşiktaş wharf

In the years since I first came to Istanbul, the public transport system has expanded from a handful of ferry lines, slow clanking suburban trains, a couple of tram lines, one underground vertical railway, public buses and privately owned dolmuş (a type of minibus), to a network of metro lines with more opening up each year, the Marmaray railway system, ferry services to more locations that better link both sides of the city, the Metrobus lines, new funiculars making it possible to travel from the shores of the Bosphorus to the crest of Istanbul's hills in a few minutes, and an expanded fleet of buses going to more destinations than even I knew existed.

As of September 2022 there were two different transport cards to choose from allowing you to use every form of transport barring dolmuş. The İstanbulkart is a good option for those planning to stay in Istanbul for more than a few weeks. Similar in size to a credit card, you can buy an İstanbulkart (Istanbul Card) when you arrive at Istanbul Airport on the European side of the city or at Sabiha Gokçen Airport on the Asian side. You can also buy them from vending machines at major bus and ferry terminals as well as peopled ticket booths. The machines have instructions in different languages

including English, something I can't guarantee if you prefer to buy from a person.

The cost for the card only was 70tl in August 2023 and then you load it up with enough money to cover your journeys. If you're travelling in a couple both of you can use the one card. Assuming you're planning to visit a lot of the places mentioned in this book, you can easily get through several hundred Turkish lira in a couple of days. When you need to add money look for the Biletmatik machines at transport hubs and freestanding small kiosks selling newspapers, cigarettes and chewing gum with the words İstanbulkart or Akbil (the card's former name) Bayii on their awnings. Some Halk Ekmek (Public Bread) booths also refill Istanbul cards.

The Istanbul City Card is a good choice for people coming to Istanbul for only a few days up to a couple of weeks. It offers unlimited transportation for 1 to 15 days, so you only pay for the number of days you know you'll use it. There's also the option to include a ride on a tour bus is you want to start your visit with an overview of the  major sites, on a tour bus if you want to start your visit with an overview of the major sites. The distinctive blue Istanbul City Card ticket machines are in more than 30 places most visited by tourists around the city, including Eminönü and Sultanahmet.

Here's a couple of things general tips for when you're out and about. The Marmaray system is very efficient but you need to keep an eye out for your stop. The announcements stating the name of approaching stations aren't always clear or audible and when the carriages are packed or you're short like me, it's easy to miss the name plates on the platforms themselves. If in doubt, ask.

Knowing what stop is coming up is easier on buses, most of the time. Buses have overhead screens inside showing a number of stops at a time, and many bus stops are modern shelters with the name of the stop visible on them. However the screens don't always work or can be out of sync with the bus so the screen says one name and the bus shelter is for the previous stop. I always screenshot the names of the bus stops leading up the stop I want, just in case. You can do this by entering the bus number you need into the İstanbul Elektrik Tramvay ve Tünel İşletmeleri (General Directorate of Istanbul Electric Tram and Tunnel Operations – or IETT for short) official bus website www.iett.istanbul/en. Click through to the 'passed stops' tab and you'll see the full list of stops along the route. One last thing to remember, in some neighbourhoods the bus stop is just a pole with a yellow sign attached. They have the name of the stop printed on them but aren't always immediately obvious.

PUBLIC TRANSPORT HUBS

For most entries in this book, the how to get there instructions are based on starting from a particular transport hub. If there isn't one close to the place you're going, I've provided the necessary information for you to reach it without too much difficulty. Here are the main transport hubs you'll need to know about.

ON THE ASIAN SIDE OF ISTANBUL

FOR KADIKÖY
Kadıköy Buses

The Kadıköy terminal for buses runs along the water front, and starts just in front of the wharf where Şehirhatları (City Line) ferries to Karaköy, Eminönü and Kabataş depart from and arrive. The bus terminal is not a structure as such, just two large areas filled with street level *peron,* platforms, and buses.

The first section, which I refer to throughout this book as **Kadıköy transport hub A**, is for buses heading inland in the direction of Minibus Yolu (what everyone calls Fahrettin Keim Gökay Caddesi) or to Sahil Yolu (official name Operatör Cemil Topulu Caddesi), along the Sea of Marmara.

The second section, further along the waterfront in the direction of Haydarpaşa Railway Station, which I refer to throughout this book as **Kadıköy transport hub B**, is for buses heading towards the E5 highway.

The two sections are divided by a one storey building with a flag pole on it, next to an enormous screen overhead listing bus and peron numbers. Behind that is an orange demountable, housing public toilets run by the İstanbul Büyükşehir Belediyesi, the Istanbul Municipality Council, or IBB for short. They're usually quite clean and as a

13

bonus you can use your Istanbul Card to enter them. Otherwise have a one Turkish Lira (1tl) coin handy.

The Havataş buses to Sabiha Gokçen Airport and Havaist buses to Istanbul Airport leave from this central spot.

Kadıköy dolmuş transport hub

Dolmuş in Kadıköy

Just beyond Kadıköy transport hub B, almost at the end of the waterfront, you come to the Kadıköy dolmuş transport hub. Dolmuş are small passenger vans that follow set routes but pick up and drop people off anywhere along the way. They often wait until they're full before departing, or at designated points along the route. Their main destinations are listed on the side of the vehicle. When you need to use a dolmuş I've written down in Turkish what you need to say or show to get to your destination. Almost any man standing around having a cigarette is a driver on a break and will be able to tell you which one you need to board. They only accept cash payments.

FOR ÜSKÜDAR

The Üsküdar transport hub is located on the edge of the Bosphorus and consists of bus stops, Şehirhatları, Dentur and Turyol ferry wharves, dolmuş stops, an underground metro service and the Marmaray commuter line that connects both sides of the city, travelling above and below ground. At first glance it seems a bit chaotic but there is an order to things which I will explain. Please note I am only including the transport services you need to access sites in this book.

Üsküdar Marmaray and Metro entrance

First up, there's a big square on the waterfront called Üsküdar Meydanı and orientation starts from there. Standing with your back to the water where a road leads inland away from the square, look across the road and you'll see an entry to the Marmaray on the corner. It's an oblong structure set on a platform with a sloped cantilevered roof identified by the words Marmaray Üsküdar Istasyonu across the front. Behind that, look for tall columns with the letter M on them, indicating the metro services. Either of these entries will take you underground to where there are turnstiles for both the metro and the Marmaray. They at different points inside the station so check you're at the correct bank of turnstiles before you register your Istanbul card and pass through to the platforms. For reference, there are IBB public toilets below ground if you need them. You'll need to follow the signs or failing that ask a security guard the way. Saying *tuvalet,* or even just the word toilet slowly and clearly, while waving your hand around to imply urgency, usually works.

Üsküdar inland bus stop

Buses heading inland and further afield from Üsküdar leave from stops lined up along the road to the right of the Marmaray entrance described above. Bus numbers as well as timetables (if you're lucky) are displayed on the bus shelters.

Üsküdar Bosphorus bus terminal

Once again, standing with your back to the Bosphorus where the square meets the road leading inland, look across the road to the left. On the corner opposite the Marmaray entry you'll see a large marble fountain close to the road. The two minarets belonging to Mihriman Sultan Camii rise up behind it. I recommend you visit the mosque if you have time. Note there are free public toilets in the mosque grounds.

Cross over to that corner (but don't enter the mosque) and walk about 50 metres further along, keeping parallel to the water. You'll come to a small bus terminal. As with Kadıköy the bus terminal isn't a structure as such. It consists of a number of bus shelters next to one another spread over several parallel lanes. Many of the buses that depart from here are smaller than average. Although people will queue up for the buses unlike elsewhere in Istanbul, order often dissolves when the doors open so getting a seat isn't guaranteed.

Üsküdar ferries

All the Şehirhatları and other ferries embarking and disembarking from Üsküdar leave from the stretch of waterfront next to Üsküdar Meydanı, starting from opposite Mihriman Sultan Camii and the Üsküdar Bosphorus bus terminal. Each ferry line destination is clearly marked, with the name of each stop they make. You can use your Istanbul Card to travel on all of them.

ON THE EUROPEAN SIDE OF ISTANBUL

FOR EMİNÖNÜ/SİRKECİ

In this book I use the term Eminönü transport hub to describe the area that starts from Sirkeci Istasyonu (Sirkeci Railway Station) and stretches along the waterfront all the way past Galata Köprüsü (Galata Bridge) to the Haliç Metro Köprüsü (Golden Horn Metro Bridge). The hub includes the international Sirkeci Railway Station, the Sirkeci Marmaray stop below it, and the tram running from Kabataş up through Sultanahmet, as well as numerous ferry services. After you walk through the Galata Bridge you come to the first stop of the Eminönü-Alibey Tramvay (Eminönü-Alibey tram line) that runs all the way up Haliç (the Golden Horn). The Eminönü

Otobüs Durağı (the Eminönü bus terminal) is another 500 metres beyond the tram station, next to the Haliç Metro Köprüsü. From this terminal you can catch buses leading to parts further afield in Istanbul. If you need to get to Yenikapı or Taksim, walk up onto the Haliç Metro Köprüsü. The metro station itself is in the middle of this cable-stayed bridge which also offers great views across the city.

Sirkeci end

As before, I'll use the water for orientation. Standing with your back to the water, Sirkeci Railway Station is across the road to the left. The station is the salmon coloured two storey brick building behind the small tree filled park. The easiest way to get to Sirkeci from Eminönü is to follow the tramline. It runs parallel to the water until it turns right and stops outside the station, before winding up the hill to Sultanahmet and beyond. To catch the Marmaray enter the railway building and continue straight on to reach the escalators and stairs leading down to the turnstiles. There are plenty of signs to guide you.

Şehirhatları Vapur

City Line ferries to the Asian side of the city and other destinations on the European side run from Eminönü. You can also take a ferry up the Bosphorus, the Eminönü-Rumelikavağı line, using your Istanbul card from here. There are many touts offering Bosphorus cruises. They're great if you have limited time and want to see Istanbul from the water. However they cost more that the Şehirhatları and only go as far as the second bridge.

Ferry turnstiles at Eminönü

Eminönü Otobüs Durağı end

When you're standing with the water at your back, the Eminönü bus terminal is to your right. You won't be able to see it from where you are but walk in that direction until you come to the Galata Bridge. There's a flight of stairs leading up onto the bridge where you can see lots of people fishing, but you want to head for the underpass that takes you to the other side of the bridge. Do note there are public toilets in the underpass but none elsewhere along the waterfront. You can pay for them using your Istanbul card. otherwise feed 1tl into the turnstiles.

When you reach the other side you'll be in what I call fish sandwich square. Colourfully decorated boats are moored alongside the quay crewed by men dressed in striped waistcoats and *fez*, frying fish for sandwiches. Each boat has their own marquee set in front of them, furnished with low tables and stools.

Keep following the shoreline with the water on your right. Just up ahead you'll see the Eminönü tram station for the Eminönü-Alibey tramway on the left. Continue on past the Turyol ferry wharf on your right. You'll reach the new Eminönü Otobüs Durağı after about 5 minutes. The bus terminal covers quite a large space and bus numbers are listed on posts or large signs on the bus shelters. However with so many buses coming and going all the time it can be a bit confusing working out where to get the bus you want. There's no information booth but I find most of the drivers happy to point me in the right direction when I can't work out where my bus departs from.

FOR SULTANAHMET

Sultanahmet is a major focus for tourism in Istanbul so I will assume the location is known to readers of this book. The only public transport available here is the Kabataş-Bağcılar tramway. The main things to know are the following. If you want to get to Sirkeci, Eminönü or closer to Beşiktaş and Dolmabahçe Palace, catch the tram in the direction of Kabataş. For the Grand Bazaar and Aksaray, a 10-minute walk from the Yenikapı Marmaray Station, catch the tram finishing up at Bağcılar. Whenever you do catch the tram be conscious of your belongings and keep your hands on them at all times, even if it means hugging your bag to your chest. The trams can get very crowded and make it easy for pickpockets to operate. If someone's standing too close to you don't be embarrassed to say something or glare at them so they know you're not an easy mark.

FOR TAKSIM

Taksim Bus and Car Tunnel

Taksim Meydanı, the big open square at the end of Istiklal Caddesi is another major tourist centre in Istanbul. Above ground the signs leading to the metro are clearly marked. Note, you also access the funicular down to Kabataş via the underground metro entrance. However the entry to the IETT Otobüs Durağı (IETT Bus Stop) is less obvious. Stand next to the metro sign with a large M on it in the square, next to a staircase leading below ground, opposite the monument dedicated to Mustafa Kemal Atatürk. Look over to your right and you'll see Gezi Park. The entrance to the IETT bus station is near the left-hand corner of the park. Less a bus terminal than a noisy, gloomy tunnel, this is where buses coming from and going to Eminönü and Karaköy pick up and set down passengers. It's a bit of a bun fight to be honest so watch where you step and keep your eyes peeled for your bus number.

OTHER PRACTICAL INFORMATION

There are plenty of guidebooks and online posts covering practical matters you need to know about to make the most of your visit to Istanbul. I suggest you do your homework before you come. Nonetheless, here are some hints and handy tips I've gleaned through living here.

These days almost every store, restaurant, cafe or bar accepts credit and debit cards. When you're shopping for keepsakes to take home, offering to pay in cash is the best way to get a discount. Do remember that while *pazarlık,* bargaining, is part of the culture, the person you're dealing with is trying to make a living, and ridiculously low offers can be seen as an insult. Have fun practising your pazarlık skills in shops selling souvenirs and at the Grand Bazaar, but don't try them when you go to buy water, bus tickets and so on. It's not done.

Be aware most Turkish bank ATMs now charge a fee when you withdraw Turkish Lira (tl) using a card from a foreign bank. The amount will be shown on the screen of the Bankomatik (the Turkish version of an ATM) and you have to accept it to proceed with the withdrawal. Likely your own bank will charge a foreign currency transaction fee too so check this in advance.

Try to hold on to low denomination notes and coins if possible. Istanbul goes through phases when no one has anything smaller than a 20tl lira note. Getting back change when you've handed over a

50tl note for a 5tl purchase often involves waiting as the shopkeeper rifles through their pockets or visits neighbouring shops. Coins come in handy for using public toilets or when you hear a great busker on a train, ferry or street corner and you want to reward them for their efforts. On the topic of toilets, if you can't find an IBB toilet and there's no mosque nearby, outside tourist heavy areas most cafe and restaurants will let you use theirs if you ask politely. Either look for the international toilet symbols for men and women or the words *bay* for man and *bayan* for woman. Through force of habit and early experiences in Turkey I still carry my own tissues and some of the individual wet wipe sachets you get given after your meals. Finding toilet paper and soap in a Turkish toilet isn't a given.

Never order food at an establishment that doesn't give you a menu, either printed out or via QR code, no matter how tired you are. If you do there is a possibility you'll be overcharged and no matter how nice the food, it leaves a bitter aftertaste. Some smaller establishments only ever have the names of food written on blackboards with no prices. From my observation most of the customers in these places are regulars who already know them. In this case it's perfectly acceptable to ask the price of each and every dish you're interested in. Don't be embarrassed to talk money, especially when it comes to food. Turks love when visitors show an appreciation of their traditional dishes and are more than happy to help you enjoy them.

Finally, enjoy discovering a little of the Istanbul I know. A place people from all walks of life and different parts of the country call home. Each of them has their own story and I hope by going to the places in *Istanbul 50 Unsung Places* you'll get to know some of them.

Iyi geziler!

MOSQUE ETIQUETTE AND OTHER RELIGIOUS MATTERS

İlahiyat Fakültesi-Marmara Üniversitesi Mosque

Many of the sites in Istanbul 50 Unsung Places are houses of worship and have great meaning to their congregations and the communities that use them. Visitors who want to enter these buildings are expected to adhere to a set etiquette. However this isn't only about taking off your shoes, covering your hair or bowing your head. It's about respect. You are entering a space where people come to grieve, commemorate their loved ones, pray for a miracle recovery, a longed for child or to seek solace for secret sorrows and despair.

If you plan to enter mosques and go inside tombs both men and women must wear clothes that cover their legs, shoulders and upper arms. Women will also need to cover their hair. I always have a headscarf in whatever bag I'm carrying for just this purpose. It also doubles as a wrap if the temperature drops, or it's summer and I'm wearing a short sleeve T-shirt or low cut top and want to cover up a bit when I find myself in a more conservative part of the city.

Wearing shoes into a mosque is not allowed. You're expected to stand on the flagstones or exposed ground in front of the entry way and remove your shoes there, without stepping onto the uncovered ground in your bare feet or socks as this will render your feet unclean. I negotiate this by taking off one shoe and stepping onto the laminate or carpet area in my bare or socked foot, and then remove the other shoe. It's tricky but manageable. There are almost always rows of wooden cupboards with small open cubicles where you can leave your shoes. These are located either side of the entry way although in some mosques they're located just inside the building. You can also carry your shoes in with you and I use a recycled plastic shopping bag (I put one in every bag I own). Depending on the design of the mosque, there can be more than one entry. Taking your shoes in with you gives you the freedom to exit from a different section of the mosque. Sadly, in recent years shoes have gone missing from mosques in busier districts. When this is the case you'll see photos of suspected thieves posted at the mosque entry with warnings not to leave your shoes outside.

When you exit, the practice is to quickly slip on your shoes and then move away and leave the path clear for others. Look out for stone benches either side of the doorway. I usually slip into my shoes as best I can, shuffle over and sit down to put on my shoes properly, especially in winter when I'm wearing lace up boots.

Entrance to mosques in Turkey is free. In the tourist centre of Sultanahmet, if you aren't appropriately clothed, or don't have a head scarf, you can purchase coverings for a fee. Outside these areas, at least when I travelled with my shorts wearing father, I was usually able to borrow something for him to wear, in many cases baggy legged trousers called *şalvar*. The sight of a man wearing women's floral pants always made the security guards laugh but Dad didn't mind. I would strongly recommend that on days when you plan to visit a mosque or tomb, you dress for the occasion. In summer light pants that end below the knee, like capris, are suitable for both men and women. Men should wear shirts with sleeves, so no muscle tops guys, and the same goes for women. You don't need to wrap down to your wrists but do make sure your shoulders are well covered and avoid low cut scoop necks or crop tops.

In my experience I've found that dressing in keeping with accepted customs earns me respect, and women in the mosques are more likely to interact with me. This is more relevant these days as in recent years in many mosques, women's sections have been created in the main prayer area where none existed in the past. In larger mosques that have always had women's sections, I'm regularly directed to them straight away, whereas in the past I was left to explore the mosque without being approached. I will still walk into the main prayer area, but I make sure not to pass in front of anyone who is praying. According to Islam a woman passing in front of a man during prayer interrupts the act and they will have to start again. I also don't take photos of people in which they are easily identified unless they are happy for me to do so. Generally people in mosques are engaged in private devotions and I don't view them as material for social media.

When you do get told to go the women's prayer sections, go for it. The advantages are varied if not always obvious. When they are small partitioned add ons you are in among women focussed on prayer and get to see what that involves. I admit to sometimes feeling a bit uncomfortable because I'm not there as a believer, but no one makes me feel like an intruder. My favourite women's sections are in Fatih Camii and Büyük Çamlica Camii. The women's section in Fatih Camii gives you a bird's eye view into the mosque interior through wooden lattices reminiscent of Ottoman times. At Büyük Çamlica, the designed for purpose balcony that wraps around three sides of the mosque is a world apart, as I've written about more extensively in my book *Longing for Istanbul: The Words I Haven't Said Yet*. Big or small, entering the women's section of a mosque gives you a different perspective on Islam and its role in everyday life.

Most mosques in Istanbul are open seven days a week with five formal prayers held a day, led by an *imam*, the religious leader of the community. Visitors are required to wait outside until they finish. You can use this time to look at the courtyard, visit the tombs and in some cases have a glass of tea at a cafe set up inside the grounds. The times are posted up outside but be aware these change throughout the year according to when the sun rises and sets. There are extra services during religious holidays like Ramazan, Şeker and Kurban Bayram and prayer sets are extended for funerals.

As a final note on mosques, almost every one I've ever been to in Istanbul has public toilets. A lot of them are free to use nowadays and although the floor might be wet, the water on it will be clean, at least in the women's toilets. Don't forget to check you have some tissues and wet wipes in your bag before you leave your accommodation in the morning and you'll be good to go. So to speak.

Istanbul is home to a handful of synagogues, some of them still active. As the majority are only open to the public one day in the year I have not included them.

Churches in Istanbul are mainly of the Greek or Armenian Orthodox faiths, with a couple of active Catholic and Protestant establishments. Each have their own rules but I have never been asked to cover my head before entering one. Entrance to the interior of Greek and Armenian churches is generally limited to Sundays and religious holy days such as Easter, Christmas and Saints' Days. These fall according to the Orthodox rather than the Gregorian Calendar as used by Protestant and Catholic faiths. Where more regular access is possible, I've noted it in the individual details for that entry. In some cases, if you are of the faith, the caretaker will let you into the church to pray outside of regular hours. I ask you not to abuse this nor take photographs inside if it is forbidden. They have legitimate concerns that need to be respected, along with their privacy. You are allowed to enter the narthex, the antechamber of the church, most days of the week.

That's it from me about mosque etiquette and other religious matters. Time to get out and explore!

ASIAN SIDE OF ISTANBUL

KADIKÖY AND SURROUNDING NEIGHBOURHOODS

Ali Muhiddin Hacı Bekir

Some of my fondest memories from the first time I lived in Istanbul in 2000 involve being in someone's car driving in search of the best. The best *lahmacun*, the best *döner*, the best *baklava*. Whatever taste sensation I craved, it didn't matter if there were six local stores selling what I wanted, we always went with a trusted recommendation, even if it meant being stuck in traffic or travelling for hours to the other side of town, across the Bosphorus or up to the end of the Golden Horn. I quickly learned to not eat just anywhere but to always ask first.

Naturally, when I wanted to purchase some Turkish Delight to take back to Australia as gifts for my family, I asked my Turkish friends where I should buy it from. The answer was unanimous. If I wanted to buy the best *lokum* as it's called in Turkish, I should head for Ali Muhiddin Hacı Bekir, or Hacı Bekir for short. I've been buying from their branch in Kadıköy ever since, with occasional forays to their stores in Eminönü and Beyoğlu. The popularity of lokum dates back centuries and features in many romantic tales involving sultans, jealous women in the harem, and the hardworking sweet makers tasked with creating something to stop them fighting. However it's widely believed the version of the sweet we know today was invented in Turkey back in the 18th century by Şekerci Bekir Efendi himself.

Mr Bekir the Sugar Maker came to Istanbul from Kastamonu in the Black Sea region of Turkey in 1777, and opened a small sweet shop. Other şekerci sold sweet treats made from a mixture of flour, *sakız,* that is mastic gum, honey and molasses, flavoured with rose petals and other natural ingredients such as cinnamon. Şekerci Bekir substituted flour for starch, an ingredient discovered by German scientist Constantin Kitchhoff in 1811. It adds that deliciously chewy texture for which lokum is famous.

After completing the Hac (Hajj in English), the religious pilgrimage to Mecca. sometime between 1817 and 1820 Mr Bekir took the honorary title Hacı, and was thenceforth known as Şekerci Haci Bekir Efendi. Over time the name Şekerci Hacı Bekir Efendi became internationally famous due to the quality of the Turkish Delight he made. The word lokum is derived from the Arabic rahat'ül hülküm, literally meaning 'comfort of the throat'. An Englishman visiting Istanbul liked these 'mouthfuls of delight' so much that he took some back home with him and introduced them as Turkish Delight to his circle of friends.

Ali Muhiddin Hacı Bekir also make boiled lollies called *akide*, candied fruit and sugared almonds. The akide are stored in tall glass jars, topped with conical lids made of thin sheets of brass or copper.

In the past these lollies were highly valued due to the exorbitant price of sugar, and the difficulty in making them due to its lack of consistency in the heating process. The development of refined sugar has made

Choosing Turkish Delight at Hacı Bekir

it easier to produce better consistency, but akide are still finicky to make. They only stay fresh for up to ten days at a time so are only produced in small batches.

The word akide also means confession of faith and gifting them was seen as a pledge of loyalty in Ottoman times. The Janissary, the royal guard of the ruling sultan, was paid every three months. If they were happy with their salary they would present a gift of mouthwatering akide to the high court officials as a sign of their fidelity to the sultan.

Sugar almonds are still given to those viewing newborns for the first time while lokum is served on the 40th and 52nd days after a death. On the first anniversary of the loss lokum is served once again in a ceremony called a *mevlit*. The shelves behind the counters in Hacı Bekir are stacked with boxes you can buy to fill with lokum or other sweet treats of your choosing. There are square padded boxes covered in luxurious swathes of velvet, colourful reproductions of early Istanbul street scenes and the ever popular more austere round wooden boxes stamped with a logo designed to celebrate the founding of the Turkish Republic.

Due to the original nature of the sweets and the care with which they were made, Hacı Bekir won the approval of the people and came to the attention of Sultan Mahmud II. Mahmud II ruled as Ottoman Sultan from 1808 until 1839 and is remembered for his passion for Westernisation and innovation. He awarded Hacı Bekir with the role of *Şekercibaşı*, head confectioner to the Ottoman Palace. When Hacı Bekir died in 1873 first his son Mehmed Muhiddin Efendi and then his grandson Ali Muhiddin Hacı Bekir, took over the position.

In his first year in charge of the business son Mehmed took the silver medal at a confectionery fair held in Vienna under the patronage of the Austro-Hungarian emperor Franz Joseph I. While at the fair Mehmed noticed participants from western countries promoted their products using brand names. On his return he created the first such name of the Ottoman Empire. At later fairs held in

Cologne in 1888, in Chicago in 1893 and then Brussels in 1897, he came home with one silver and then two gold medals. His son Ali, Hacı Bekir's grandson, followed in the family footsteps, winning gold medals at fairs in Paris and Nice. He too was awarded the title of Şekercibaşı for the Ottoman Palace as well as for the Egyptian Palace in 1911 and then went on to open Hacı Bekir branches in Cairo and Alexandria.

Before they renovated their store in Kadıköy they had original certificates from some of these competitions framed and hanging up on the walls. They've since been moved but the lovely curved glass front windows are still in place. I always stop at the high counters and chat with the staff I've known for more than a decade before selecting one or two, OK, I admit it, usually three pieces of Turkish Delight to have with a coffee. Depending on my mood I might have a Turkish coffee or a double espresso. Either way, they're very good. After the Kadıköy store reopened I was thrilled to see they had kept the simple yet elegant black and white tiles on the floor and added comfortable seating, creating an oasis of calm in the middle of the ever busy Kadıköy Çarşı. Sitting at the back of the shop, looking up at the high wooden ceilings, it's easy to daydream about the families that might have once lived in this former Rum house.

I've tried many different types of Turkish Delight but *badem ezmesi* are my favourite. So much so that whenever I'd buy a few boxes to take back for my family, I'd always start off by getting the mixed selection. Badem ezmesi are more expensive than the other lokum and I wanted my family to have the best. Technically speaking they're actually marzipan and I'd start to wonder, would my family really know enough about what goes into them to appreciate the difference from the more traditional versions made from rose water or nuts? Unfailingly I'd end up giving them the better-known selections and they loved them. If my visit coincided with Christmas the box of Turkish Delight would empty almost as soon as they managed to remove the wrapping paper. As for the badem ezmesi, Kim and I would consume them with coffee, in a solemn ritual ensuring neither of us ate more pieces than the other. We each took one of the same type at the same time, so it was completely and absolutely fair. That's if you consider having to share something so delightful fair.

When I think of lokum I only think of Ali Muhiddin Haci Bekir, with good reason. The Hacı Bekir family have maintained the same high standards set by Hacı Bekir back in 1777, through six generations right to this day.

Address: Muvakkithane Caddesi No 6/1, Kadıköy

To visit my local Ali Muhiddin Hacı Bekir, from Söğütlü Çeşme Caddesi turn right into Mühürdar Caddesi that leads through the heart of the Kadıköy shopping centre. The second street on the right is Muvakkithane Caddesi. Haci Bekir is on the left, towards the bottom.

Other branches at:

İstiklal Caddesi No 83/A, Beyoğlu (just down from Taksim)

Hamidiye Caddesi No 31-33, Eminönü (near the Yeni Camii)

Opening times: 08.00-21.00, 7 days a week

Aya Efimia Rum Ortodoks Kilisesi

Like many of the churches still active in Istanbul, the exterior walls of Saint Euphemia Church in the heart of Kadıköy's busy shopping centre give no indication of what's inside. Most days of the week it's only possible to enter the narthex. In the past this antechamber was as far as people doing penance for their sins or those preparing for baptism or confirmation, known as catechumen, could enter. The marble slabs on the floor and walls, a holy spring dedicated to Saint Paraskevi, several sarcophagi and a silver plated icon of Saint Euphemia create a space radiating calm, especially when compared to the bustle outside.

The serenity is alluring but also somewhat deceptive once you know the history of the church. It's dedicated to a woman called Euphemia, the daughter of a senator named Philophronos and his wife Theodosia. They were both Christians and lived in Chalcedon, present day Kadıköy. When she was a teenager Euphemia dedicated herself to a life of perpetual virginity in the service of God and was consecrated to virginity by the church. When Priscus, the governor of Chalcedon, ordered all inhabitants of the city attend a pagan festival and offer sacrifices to Ares the Greek God of War, Euphemia was one of 49 Christians who hid themselves and carried out Christian prayer services.

They were all arrested and subject to various methods of torture in order to make them recant. Hoping to intimidate her into confessing by separating the young believer from her companions, Priscus kept Euphemia back when he sent the others to be tried by Emperor Diocletian. Euphemia stayed strong in her faith so Priscus had her tied to a wheel set with sharp knives. Still she kept silent so he commanded she be thrown into a fiery oven. The first two soldiers tasked with the job, Sosthenes and Victor, claimed to see two angels in the midst of the flames and refused to follow orders. They declared themselves Christians and were punished for their faith in God rather than the governor by being thrown into an arena in Chalcedon to be devoured by wild animals. Accepting their fate they prayed to God and died untouched.

The next two soldiers decided to do as they were told and cast Euphemia to the flames. Ever stoic she prayed to God for mercy and her prayers were answered. When she walked out unscathed Priscus' rage knew no bounds. It became clear to him that Euphemia would not forsake Christianity, so he had her thrown to the lions in the same arena where her would be rescuers had perished.

According to legend, the lions refused to kill Euphemia, licking her instead. Wild bears were then sent into the arena to attack her and one of them, a she-bear, bit Euphemia on the leg. The wound was only small but she died instantly. At the moment of her death an earthquake struck, causing terror in the guards and spectators who all fled. Her parents took advantage of the ensuing panic and removed Euphemia's body to a safe place nearby where they buried their beloved daughter. It was the year 303AD, the first year of the Great Persecution of Christians under the Roman emperor Diocletian.

Euphemia died on September the 16th, was declared a saint and even after drawing her last breath continued to play an important role in the church. At the 4th Ecumenical Council held in Chalcedon in 451 AD, 630 high ranking bishops met to debate the essence of Jesus Christ. Was he altogether divine as the Monophysites believed or was he both human and divine, as per Orthodox faith? Two tomes, one outlining Orthodox belief, the other the belief of the Monophysites, were placed in the same spot inside Euphemia's casket. When it was opened sometime later the volume belonging to the Monophysites had moved and was under her feet. Understood as a miracle, this event is remembered on July the 11th each year.

Euphemia's sarcophagus was made of either gold or silver, depending on who you believe. Whatever the material, her holy presence attracted crowds of pilgrims who came to pray at her tomb. The original structure was looted and destroyed in the 7th century during the Persian invasions of around 615 or 626. According to legend, Saint Euphemia's bones were transferred across the water to Constantinople as the European side of Istanbul was then known for safe keeping, but were thought to be lost forever when they were thrown into the sea.

However they were recovered and hidden on the Island of Lemnos until Byzantine Empress Irene ordered they be returned to the city in 796AD. She had them placed in the Church of Haghia Euphemia, the converted Palace of Antiochus at the Hippodrome in Sultanahmet. The church once contained a series of frescoes documenting the life of Euphemia and the Forty Martyrs of Sebasteia and military saints but it was severely damaged in the 13th and again in the 15th centuries. Knowledge of it all but disappeared until 1939 when fragments of the frescoes came to light. Finds from archaeological digs over the following two decades are now housed in the Istanbul Archaeological Museum.

Saint Euphemia was commonly known as the 'all-praised' in the Orthodox Church, and her bones were moved from the sarcophagus after a fire in the 16th century. They were taken to the Aya Yorgi Rum Kilisesi ve Fener Rum Patrikhanesi, Saint George's Church and Ecumenical Patriarchate otherwise known as the Eastern Orthodox Cathedral, where they remain today. The present day Saint Euphemia Church started life as a church attached to the monastery of Saint Vassi in 1694. Many icons and articles of faith dating to Byzantine times are still in use in the church.

If you come on a Sunday to attend a service, once inside the main body of the church you'll see it has a Greek cross layout, a common feature of Byzantine architecture. Marble columns stand guard in front of a richly decorated iconostasis, while the interior is bathed in gauzy light coming in from the small dome above, mixing with smouldering incense. It bounces off cut glass chandeliers, crucifixes, Corinthian columns, shiny wooden pews and pulpits, and icons gleaming with gold leaf and silver plate. A small but devout congregation sits and chants amongst small oil portraits of pensive saints while scenes from the life of Christ are depicted in frescoes on the ceiling surfaces above. Visitors are welcome to enter but do remember this is a place of worship and act accordingly.

Address: Yasa Caddesi No 27, Kadıköy (at the intersection with Mühürdar Caddesi in the pedestrian section known as Kadıköy Çarsı)

If you've come over to Kadıköy by boat from Eminönü, Kabataş or Karaköy, once you've disembarked stand so the water is behind you. Look straight ahead and you'll see a wide traffic filled road heading up a hill. That's Söğütlü Çeşme Caddesi. Cross over so you're walking on the right-hand side of this street and turn right at Mühürdar Caddesi. Saint Euphemia Church is one block in.

Ayios Yeorgios Rum Ortodoks Kilisesi

Over the last decade or so Yeldeğirmeni in Kadıköy has been undergoing gentrification. Students, creatives, foreign tourists and residents have been begun to move in, attracted by family run corner shops, Italian and German designed apartment blocks and former schools, offering a slower more leisurely slice of life compared to elsewhere in Istanbul. Previously Yeldeğirmeni was a modest residential neighbourhood with a population of Turks, Jews, Rum, Armenians and those of European ancestry. This mix reflected the original demographics of Constantinople and the addition of expert artisans brought over to the city to work on construction of the Haydarpaşa Railway Station.

Each group had their own place of worship and the Ayios Georgios Greek Orthodox Church was where the Rum went to pray. Until 1919 the site where the church now stands only contained a school, believed to date from around 1881. The school moved to the three-storey building next door and the original building was then used as a church. That building was demolished in 1927 and the present church erected in its place.

The interior is packed with religious paintings, a glowing iconostasis, icons, delicate polycandelon and chandeliers gleaming through the incense. Saint George and the Dragon feature throughout, including on the altar cloth brought out during services. A small pulpit covered in golden mosaics is particularly of note. It's decorated with portraits and scenes from the lives of the saints and attached to a single column. The columns themselves are fairly plain, but the column heads are carved with the cross and stylised fronds. The interior is quite tiny, with seats for the congregation ranged around the perimeter walls and also in a smaller section in the centre. If you are able to enter please be respectful of other peoples' beliefs and space. The last time I went I stood quietly at the rear and listened as the priest sang the service. They don't allow photography inside the church itself but are happy for you to photograph the narthex and grounds.

Outside in the garden there's a 15-metre-high bell tower. It's made from iron and the legs are actually lengths of train track. It was erected to hold a bell poured and mounted by Samatyalı Zilciyan Usta, the most famous master bell maker of the time.

Address: Karakolhane Caddesi No 60, Yeldeğirmeni

Traffic is always heavy in Kadıköy so the quickest way to get to Yeldeğirmeni is to walk up the wide traffic filled road heading up the hill from the ferry wharves. That's Söğütlü Çeşme Caddesi. Just before Boğa, the statue of a bull, turn left and walk along Halitağa Caddesi. Follow this pedestrian street until it opens up to traffic and cross the road into Karakolhane Caddesi. The church is another five minutes along, on the right-hand side.

Opening times: Sunday during services and at announced times during the week. You'll have to chance your luck but Yeldeğirmeni itself is well worth a wander.

Barış Manço Evi

The first type of music I heard when I came to Turkey was Arabesque. Its Arabic strains and songs about loss and longing were hugely popular and Ibrahim Tatlıses was the king. He made his first cassette tape in 1970, the same year musician Barış Manço released a single called *Dağlar, dağlar* (Mountains, mountains). *Dağlar, dağlar* became a massive hit, selling 700,000 copies, no mean feat when you remember this was back when fans had to go to a shop and buy an actual record. There were no cheap and easy downloads then. Manço began playing music in his teens and went on to write 200 songs in his lifetime. Over the years his look morphed from long-haired hippy in nubuck coats and chunky hand knitted cardigans to stereotypical 1970s rocker, sporting a wispy moustache, skin-tight flares and long hair.

Briefly touching on Tatlıses again, he's not to everyone's taste but I really like his voice and the memories his music evokes of my travels throughout Turkey, particularly to the east and south east where he was born. I was less enamoured of what I knew of Manço's style, a synthesis of Turkish rock and folk music known as Anatolian Rock. I associated him with the guitar driven solos of 1970s rockers my brother loved to practice that bored me to tears.

Then I visited Barış Manço Evi, the Baris Manço Museum housed in his former residence on the

Asian side of Istanbul, in the leafy streets of Moda. The building is one of two identical structures commissioned for an Englishman named Dawson, designed by Rum architect Constantin Pappa. Manço bought the house in 1984 and carefully restored it. Now the lavish rooms are a showcase for a diverse range of splendid items from his private life and professional ventures. It's packed with paraphernalia of his music career such as costumes, tour photos, and prizes and ornaments gifted to Manço from people all around the world, over the course of his life.

Just off the entryway in the dining room, a 90kg French bronze chandelier hangs from the ceiling, dominating the pieces of solid European furniture arranged around the room. Manço's collection of highly ornate etched liquor glasses finished in gold and other glassware are on display in the cabinets. Next door the costume room is bursting with presents he received such as the vibrant patterned clothes, belts and accessories from his 17-city tour of Japan. These include the Chinese embroidered jacket he donned on his wedding day on 18 July 1978 and graduation outfit he wore when presented with a PhD from Haceteppe University on 19 June 1982. The walls are hung with photos and my favourite shows him decked out in jewellery, long hair flowing lushly, wearing a white jumpsuit circa 1973, the very epitome of the rocker persona.

The Steinway piano he called 'My dream' takes pride of place in the main salon while a staircase, previously painted to resemble a keyboard, leads up to rooms once used by his family. Now they hold mementoes of Manço's life and work and it's here I learned his legacy encompasses much more than his music. At one time he worked as a graphic artist and the walls are covered in examples of his work. Judging by the quality he was very talented, and it's obvious his passion for art spilled over into other aspects of his life. He designed his own costumes including many accessories. An array of dazzling bejewelled leather belts is on show in a cabinet shaped like a cello split in half. The truly amazing rings he acquired over the course of his travels, including a wonderfully elaborate dragonfly number with a stone inset to form the belly of the insect, are contained within a display cabinet shaped like a huge ring.

Music was always in his life so there are display cases packed with handwritten notes, cassettes, singles and his record albums as well as mementos from the Kurtalan Ekspres, the rock band he fronted in the 70s. Several rooms are dedicated to his time as TV producer and the host of 'From 7 to 77'. This was a music, documentary and chat show aimed at audiences aged 7 to 77, as the name suggests. The first one aired in 1988 on TRT1, the Turkish state television channel, and over the next eight years Manço travelled to almost 150 countries, introducing the world to Turkey. Right from the beginning the show was incredibly popular, especially the segment called Whizz Kid where he talked directly to children on set. Old footage shows tiny kids, some only four or five years old, singing intensely or asking important questions. Manço treated them like equals, listening carefully to their words and gave serious, well thought out replies. It was this human side of Barış Manço as much as his music that made him so well-liked and known throughout the country, regardless of people's individual musical tastes. No doubt almost every Turkish kid in the early 1990s wanted to be a Whizz Kid.

Naturally the Whizz Kid Room in the museum is by far the most popular room for Turkish visitors. Even though I didn't grow up with the show it was great to watch nostalgic adults journey back in time to their childhood. I could feel their joy as they watched episodes from the show, exclaimed over memories and put their head through the holes in blown up images so they could take selfies with the great man himself.

Tosun Yusuf Mehmet Barış Manço, to give him his full name, died on the 31st of December 1999. His diary still lies on the desk where he worked, open on that date. In it, one of his children wrote, "Babam öldü". My father is dead. Yet the extraordinary life of this in many ways ordinary unassuming man lives on in his music and images, and of course, in the memories of his legions of fans.

Address: Yusuf Kamil Paşa Sokak No 5, Moda, Kadıköy

The easiest way to get to the museum is via Bahariye Caddesi. From the ferry wharves take the wide traffic filled road called Söğütlü Çeşme Caddesi that heads up the hill. At the top you'll see a statue of a bull. To the right is the pedestrian road known locally as Bahariye Caddesi. A tram line runs through the middle of it. Follow the street all the way along until you get to the square at the end, with a metal sculpture in the middle. Walk diagonally across it to the other side and then continue along Şair Nefi Sokak. You'll see the tram track and Moda Ilkokul, a primary school, on your left. Continue on until you see a football court on your right (so don't turn right when the tram track does). The next street on the right is Yusuf Kamil

Paşa Sokak. Turn here and when you reach a front garden full of sculptures of giant tomatoes, capsicums and eggplants, with a Daewoo parked alongside them, you've arrived. The vegetables are a reference to his popular song, *Domates Biber Patlıcan* and the car was his, license plate 34 BM 777.

Opening times: 09.00-16.00, Tue-Sun. Closed Mondays & public holidays. Entry fee 20tl.

Haydarpaşa İngiliz Mezarlığı

Wherever you travel in Istanbul, just down the street on foot or across the water by ferry, you'll find a place teeming with vitality. Students, workers, parents, lovers, you name it, everyone's making the most of their time because life is short, isn't it? There's no better reminder of this than cemeteries. I'm a long time fan of them but you don't have to be a taphophile, politely known as a cemetery enthusiast or my less preferred term, a tombstone tourist, to get something out of a visit to Haydarpaşa English Cemetery.

Tucked away on the slopes up behind the port of Harem on the Asian side of Istanbul, Haydarpaşa English Cemetery dates back to 1855 when the Turkish Government gave the site to the British government during the Crimean War. The war was sparked by a dispute over the rights of Christian minorities in Palestine and saw Russia lose to an alliance between the Ottoman Empire, the UK, France and Piedmont-Sardinia. It lasted from

October 1853 to February 1956 and around 6000 soldiers who went to fight are interred in this cemetery. Sadly most of them died as the result of a cholera epidemic that swept through Istanbul at the time, rather than their wounds. The epidemic originated in India in 1847 and then spread across to Iran, Georgia, Turkey and Europe. Most likely the Crimean War played a big part in that.

Haydarpaşa Cemetery is closely associated with Florence Nightingale, otherwise known as the 'Lady with the Lamp'. During the war Ms Nightingale worked at Selimiye Barracks, the large building north of the cemetery. At night she and her cordon of nurses would go from bed to bed checking on the well-being of injured soldiers, with only flickering lamp light to guide the way. Much has been made of her calming presence as she tended to the many wounded and dying men in the barracks, but she's better remembered for introducing rigorous scientific methods into nursing such as systematic treatment and rigorous hygiene standards.

Twelve years after the cemetery first opened, British civilian burials were also allowed in the site and during the First World War, the Turks used the cemetery for the burial of Commonwealth Prisoners of War. After the Armistice, when Istanbul was occupied by the Allies from 1918 until the last of the Allied troops left the city on October 1923, further burials took place here.

The first section only contains a handful of graves and the imposing Crimean War Memorial Obelisk.

Stop a moment to admire the roses and read the plaque dedicated to Florence. One little chapel sits near a stand of trees all on its own. Inside there's a small wooden altar and two low chairs. Walk across the lawns and you come to the war graves set out in neat rows on the left. Although I'm not a fan of war history, viewing military graves and learning how the occupants came to be laid to rest so far from home taught me things about the First World War I didn't learn at school. When I was a teenager the curriculum was predominantly White, male and English.

Haydarpaşa Cemetery contains the graves of nearly one hundred and fifty Hindu, Muslim and Sikh POW soldiers of the Indian Army. They were sepoys, serving under British or other European orders in the Mesopotamia campaign, in what is now modern-day Iraq. Over the course of the war close to 675,000 Indian fighting troops as well as hundreds of thousands of auxiliary troops were involved in campaigns on the Mesopotamian front. When General Townshend's troops surrendered in April 1916, the POWs were marched all the way from Mesopotamia to POW camps in Turkey. Those who survived were held in camps in Afyonkarahisar (black poppy castle) a mountainous inland region in western Turkey.

These men were originally laid to rest in Mashlak and Osmanieh Muslim Cemeteries in Istanbul. In 1961 when those cemeteries could no longer be maintained, their remains were moved to Haydarpaşa. The ashes of the Hindus, whose remains were cremated in accordance with their faith, were scattered near the memorial commemorating their service, while their comrades of Muslim faith were re-interred here. Hard stone plaques give their names and basic details, softened here and there by fragrant shrubs of *biberiye,* rosemary, the emblem of remembrance.

However it's what you can learn from the ordinary graves that fascinates me the most. They're all spread out on well-tended sloping laws, interspersed by large trees that cast weird shapes and shadows with their branches. Some of them, the smaller ones, remember the much loved only child or even several children from the same family of diplomats, posted to a consulate in Pera (as Beyoğlu was once called). They also died as a result of the cholera epidemic and are an unfortunate early example of the collateral damage of war.

Other graves, such as that of Arthur and Rhodie Tully, are initially eye-catching for the emotion they express through the design. The Tullys were laid to rest side by side, their hearts connected by marble hearts, reflecting their love of each other and of God, their courage and intelligence and of course, their mortality. Arthur Patrick Thomas Aloysius Tully described himself as an Irishman and a British subject. In 1919 he published the first edition of what was planned as a fortnightly newspaper called Gözcü: The Observer of Constantinople. Arthur was also known as Arif Pertev Bey, and as far as the British government was concerned, he was a Turkish mouthpiece. Rhodie Tully was a champion of the abilities of Ottoman women to work as clerks in the nineteenth century at a time when only non-Turkish women were allowed to work in offices.

In amongst all the very English names are others from Hungary, Germany and Poland. Such as Marian Langiewicz, a Polish patriot and a military leader during the Polish January Uprising against the Russians in 1863. His success against the Russian forces led to members of the resurrection offering to set him up as a dictator of the revolutionary regime and he said yes. Ultimately however, the Russians were victorious and Langiewicz fled to Austria where he was caught and sent to jail. After his release he lived in Switzerland for a time before coming to Turkey. He entered into the service of the Ottoman Empire where he was known as 'Langie Bey' and died in 1887.

Then there's the grave of Jack Whitall of the wealthy Levantine family of Izmir. He died in Moda, a neighbourhood of Kadıköy, in 1904. When I mentioned the name to Ibrahim, the friendly gardener who gave me a lift through the grounds in his work golf cart, he told me there's still a Whitall woman on the daughter's side living in Moda. Through marriage she no longer bears the Whitall name but comes to the cemetery every year. She's quite old now so she rings Ibrahim and says "I'm coming" and he waits at the entry gates for her to arrive by taxi, then he transports her to the family grave. This woman wants to be buried in the cemetery but it's not open to new occupants, so to speak, only to descendants of people already buried in the grounds. Although family, she doesn't have the documents necessary to prove it. Ibrahim added that he's been working at Haydarpaşa English Cemetery for 30 years and they've only buried nine or ten people in that time.

There are too many graves to mention them all, but the one that intrigues me the most belongs to a Captain H. E. Smith of the Ship Chalmers. He died in June 1855 so could have been a victim of cholera, but his grave is set down a gentle slope, separate from his compatriots. It's markedly different too because his tombstone is Islamic in style, but carved with flowers rather than topped with a turban as would be usual for the grave of a Muslim man. Confusing matters further the inscription is the familiar Christian statement, "The lord gave and the Lord hath taken'. I wonder, why was Captain Smith placed in a corner all on his own, as if banished? Why does his headstone feature a Christian quote with Islamic symbols designed for a woman? It's possible he was a convert or preferred the company of Turks and was shunned by his own kind. Perhaps the gravestone was chosen by his Turkish canim who hoped one day to be laid to rest beside the man she loved. For now I'll just have to keep wondering.

Address: Selimiye, Üsküdar

Despite its official address, the easiest way to get to the cemetery is to catch a ferry to Kadıköy. Keeping the water on your left, walk along Rıhtım Caddesi, the waterfront road, and when you come to a bridge, continue over it. The bridge is the start of Tıbbiye

Caddesi which leads up a hill. It passes a hospital with large grounds bounded by an iron fence painted black. When you come to the end of the fence, at the corner of Burhan Felek Caddesi, turn left. You'll see a lovely example of Ottoman Nationalist architecture on the right. That's the Marmara University Law Faculty. Follow the road down. It veers slightly to the left and you'll you come to a roundabout. The entry to the cemetery is directly opposite on the other side.

Opening Times: 08.00-16.00 Mon-Fri. Closed weekends & public holidays.

Kadıköy Sineması

Even though you might end up watching a film in one language you don't understand with subtitles in Turkish that don't help either, it's worth buying a ticket just to see the main hall of the Kadıköy Cinema. It's looks exactly like I imagine the interior of a giant sea shell would appear. A massive space with huge wide striations arching across the ceiling, slightly curved to better catch and bounce off sound. It was designed by architect Melih Kotay in 1964. The Turkish press hailed it as Turkey's most modern theatre with an audience capacity of 300, a huge stage and generous facilities for actors and performers with much made of the toilets, showers and changing rooms. When it was completed the cinema won awards in Italy for its acoustic features and incredible futuristic design.

These days they have regular screenings as well as serving as a venue for film festivals throughout the year. In order to allow as many people to attend and see films from around the world, Kadıköy Cinema participates in Askıda Bilet. It's a form of paying it forward where anyone can buy a ticket to be given free to a person who can't afford the price. It derives from a tradition known as *askıda ekmek*, 'bread on the hook', where customers can pay for a loaf of bread to be hung on a hook ready to be distributed to someone unable to buy their own.

Address: General Asım Gündüz Caddesi, Kadıköy Pasajı No 25, Kadıköy

The cinema is a short walk along Bahariye Caddesi, the nickname for the wide pedestrian street named after a general, leading off from an intersection called Altıyol, six streets, although it's more commonly just called Boğa. That's bull in Turkish, in reference to the life size statue of one that marks this popular meeting place in Kadıköy. From the Kadıköy waterfront look for the wide street heading up the hill. The bull is located at the top and you'll find the entrance to the cinema about 350m further along, on the left-hand side.

Kurukahveçi Mehmet Efendi

When you visit Istanbul as a tourist, tea is usually the first beverage that comes to mind if you're thirsty. Or even when you're not because let's face it, small tulip-shaped glasses of this ruby coloured potion appear everywhere. That's because it's an essential accompaniment to just about anything you care to mention, be it important business deals or just catching up with friends. However I prefer coffee. Not just any brand mind you. For me it has to be from Kurukahveçi Mehmet Efendi, Turkey's most famous coffee producer.

The original Mehmet Efendi began working in his father's shop on Tahmis Sokak in Eminönü. Dad Hasan Efendi sold spices and green coffee beans. When Mehmet took over in 1871 he started to roast the raw coffee beans, a first for the industry in Turkey.

This initiative and interest in innovation set the tone for the company. After Mehmet Efendi's death in 1931, the business passed to his three sons, Hasan Selahattin Bey, Hulusi Bey and Ahmet Rıza Bey. The eldest son Hasan Selahattin recognised the importance of the international market and began marketing Turkish coffee abroad as well as domestically. Son Hulusi introduced mass production of roasted coffee and commissioned Zühtü Başar, a famous architect of the period, to design headquarters for the company in the Art Deco style on the site of the original family shop. Tucked behind the Egyptian Bazaar and somewhat obscured by the surrounding buildings, this striking structure remains the company's headquarters to this day. If you're in the neighbourhood stop and take in the queue of people along Hasircioğlu Sokak patiently waiting to purchase a bag of freshly ground coffee. The line never ends as new customers take their place almost as soon as someone pays and leaves.

The company began to package its roasted-ground coffee in parchment paper and distribute it to groceries and corner stores all over the city using the firm's own fleet of automobiles. This had never been done in Turkey before and was another first for Kurukahveçi Mehmet Efendi. Sales grew, leading youngest son Ahmet Rıza to realise that a popular coffee needed a recognisable logo. He'd been educated abroad and understood the power of advertising. In 1933 he commissioned Ihap Hulusi Bey, one of the city's leading graphic designers, to design a logo for the company. The eye catchingly simple Art Deco logo Hulusi Bey created is still in use today. However Kurukahveçi Mehmet Efendi didn't stop there. They developed their business further by promoting their product through posters and calendars, a revolutionary advertising idea at the time.

I buy my coffee from the Kadıköy Kurukahveçi Mehmet Efendi. It's also housed in an Art Deco style building. It opened in 1966 and is their only other shop than the original one in Eminönü. Given its position on Söğütlü Çeşme Caddesi, it's easy for fans of architecture to easily appreciate the overall design. As well as selling traditional ground Turkish coffee or whole beans, they have a range of coffee types and styles including my favourite, Columbian Filter. I've been coming for more than twenty years and most of the staff members I first dealt with still work here. I love the continuity and the fact that throughout, the quality has remained the same. The only significant change I've seen is they now accept payment via card rather than cash only as in the past. It's one of the few positives to come out of Covid.

Address: Söğütlüçeşme Caddesi 12, Kadıköy (my local) and the original at Tahmis Sokak No 66, Eminönü

Opening times for both: 08.30-19.30, 7 days a week

Meşhur Dondurmacı Ali Usta

From the moment they opened their doors in 1969, people have been lining up to buy ice cream at Meşhur Dondurmacı Ali Usta, the famous master Ali ice creamery. The master in question is Ali Kumbasar who started his training when he was only a boy. Ali Usta's ice cream is made fresh every day the Turkish way, using a natural gum called *mastic* and *salep*. Mastic is what gives Turkish ice cream that slightly chewy texture and makes it stretchy, and salep is a flour made from a type of wild orchid root. It has a creamy nutty taste. Both are mixed with fresh fruit or ingredients such as cacao, vanilla and other natural flavourings. There are even three diet varieties available, chocolate, plain and seasonal fruit, and the taste and textures of all of them are irresistible.

There are 70 different taste sensations in their range and on any given day you'll have at least 30 to 35 to choose from. Choosing ice cream is serious business in Turkey and everyone has their favourite. I'm of the belief that if you're going to have an ice cream it should be as far removed from healthy sounding tastes as possible so opt for flavours like chocolate and caramel. Then again, I love nuts so often pick hazelnut, pistachio or almond. That said, I'm rather partial to fruits of the forest like blueberries and raspberries because when I was growing up in Australia they weren't readily available and if they were, my mum never bought them because they were too expensive. I really like the banana and their Stracciatella is pretty good too. I'm greedy so I say yes when they ask if I want chocolate with crushed nuts sprinkled on top, but it's up to you.

Whether I'm in an ice cream shop or looking at a restaurant menu, the larger the selection the harder time I have trying to decide what I want so when I learned how to ask for '*iki top, yarım yarım*" I was ecstatic. Translated it means 'two scoops, half and half' so I get to pick four different flavours. Looking back at what I've just said you might think I've tried all them but I haven't. I'm yet to try Ali Usta's famous Santa Maria mix, made to a secret recipe he won't divulge to anyone. Maybe I'll try it next time.

Address: Moda Caddesi No 264, Moda, Kadıköy

There's only one Ali Usta shop, in Moda, and it's worth the walk up from Kadıköy wharf. The easiest way to get there is to head to Söğütlü Çeşme Caddesi, the wide traffic filled street leading up the hill away from the water. Walk about 200 along on the right-hand side until you come to the Çarşı bus stop. On the corner you'll see a Simit Sarayı shop. Turn right here and when you reach the small square 40 metres further on, turn left and head straight up. Once you get to the T intersection at the top turn right. This street runs into Moda Caddesi and you need to follow it almost to the end. Do note that a large part of this walk is through streets designated pedestrians only but in reality you need to watch out for motorbikes, delivery vans and cleaning vehicles.

Ali Usta is open year round and in summer you can take your cup or cone and sit outside under the trees or remain snugly warm sitting inside on a wintry day. It's such a quintessential part of any visit to Kadıköy I've even seen *gelin,* in full bridal get up, waiting in the queue.

Müze Gazhane

Hasanpaşa Gazhane opened as the Kadıköy Gas Company operated by French industrialist Charles Georges in 1892 to store and supply gas for lighting and power. Theses gasworks in Hasanpaşa were the second to be built on the Anatolian side of the city and the last to be opened in Istanbul. The Kadıköy Gas Company contract was renewed in 1924 for another 50 years, then seven years later control was transferred to the İstanbul Elektrik Şirketi, the Istanbul Electricity Company. Initially privately owned, the Istanbul Electricity Company was nationalised in 1931 and ran the gas works until they were handed over to the İstanbul Elektrik Tramvay ve Tünel İşletmeleri (IETT) in 1945. The gas works were finally closed down in 1993 along with others in the city, when authorities recognised the technology was harmful to the environment and humans. The area became a parking garage for buses belonging to the IETT and a coal storage and warehouse facility. Eventually the buildings were left empty and abandoned.

In 2015 the Istanbul Municipality Council decided to convert the space into a cultural centre and Gazhane Museum opened on July 9, 2021. It's a place where local residents and those from further afield can come together to engage in new activities, listen to concerts, explore urban Istanbul and experience the history of Kadıköy first hand.

Gazhane combines the majesty of 19th century industrial architecture, emphasising the lines and sheen of the steel and other metals used in the structures, with whimsical larger than life sculptures erected in the grounds. It's common to see children (and adults too) touch, climb and embrace the figurative and abstract pieces. A small cafe provides an assortment of drinks and snacks, and there's plenty of seating fashioned from railway sleepers for people to just hang out and not consume. Patches of grass beckon those who want to stretch out while the spongy material covering the ground makes it safe for kids to run wild.

A cinema club meets in a room off the underground floor of a parking station, beneath an enormous former liquid gas storage tank frame that now houses a concert hall. In the next tank above a smaller stage, there's a permanent display of Turkish caricatures, including *kara mizah,* political commentary in cartoon form. There are open air performances by singers, conceptual artists and dance bands during the day and in the evenings throughout the summer months. A library, study areas, a science centre and free workshops for kids and adults, including knitting, science and exercise sessions operate in repurposed buildings around the site year round, along with a multitude of other events and things to do.

Address: Kurbağalıdere Caddesi No 125, Hasanpaşa, Kadıköy

Müze Gazhane is about a 25-minute walk from the ferry wharves at the Kadıköy. Walk up the hill to Boğa and then turn left and walk down the hill past dozens of shops selling wedding dresses. At the bottom continue straight on passing under the train line. You'll see a large building surrounded by gardens on the right. That's the Kadıköy Council building. Keep going and look out for brown signs pointing the way to Müze Gazhane. A bit further on you'll see Hasanpaşa Mosque on the right. Continue straight on for another 4-5 minutes and you'll see the grey steel entry gates to the museum complex on your left. Hasanpaşa is a low-key area as yet untouched by gentrification.

If you don't want to walk you can catch the 8A bus from Kadıköy transport hub A and get out at the Hasanpaşa bus stop, a 2-minute walk from the entrance of Müze Gazhane.

Opening times for the various areas and places in the museum are as follows;

Gazhane Square: 09.00-22.00, 7 days a week
Beltur restaurant and cafe: 10.00-22.00, 7 days a week
Istanbul Bookshop: 11.00-22.00, 7 days a week
Afife Batur Library, Group study areas: 24 hours a day, 7 days a week
Climate Museum, Children's Science Museum, Caricature and Humour Museum, Gazhane Gallery 09.00-18.00, Tue-Fri, 10.00-18.00, weekends, closed Mondays.

Nayike Elgün relief sculpture

Whenever I catch the bus from my home to Kadıköy, I get off at the Kadıköy Çarşı stop. It's down the bottom of the hill once you pass Boğa, the famous statue of a bull. The Çarşı stop is beside a little triangle shaped area decorated with a few trees and bench seats populated by Turkish men engaged in the traditional male past time of sitting around doing nothing much. A money exchange place that's been there forever, a pedestrian lane, two side streets and a large bank building are located around the perimeter. Usually I cut straight through it on the way to see my computer guy then one day, for no reason I can recall, I suddenly noticed a two dimensional relief sculpture on the wall.

On it there's a woman wearing a brimless hat and glasses, standing on a platform reading from a piece of paper she holds in her hands. She's surrounded by children holding up placards saying things such as *"Azarlanmamak"* and *"Isteriz"*, meaning 'to not be scolded' and 'we want' and there's a small group of men and women watching them.

Detail from Nakiye Elgün

It made me curious. Who was this woman and what was going on? Once back home I began researching and discovered it was dedicated to Nakiye Elgün, a teacher and school director who was one of the first woman to be elected to parliament in Turkey, and a champion of the rights of women and children. Her career began during the Ottoman Empire in the late 19th century and continued on through the founding of the Turkish Republic. In 1916 she went to Syria to set up teacher training programs and during the

Turkish War of Independence of 1919 to 1923, hid ammunition in the basement of the Istanbul high school where she was the director. She was a contemporary of the famous activist and author Halide Edip and was beside her in Taksim Square where both made speeches on January 13, 1920. Elgün called on women to sacrifice for their country and to send their sons to fight. It was also in Taksim Square that Elgün presented the Geneva Declaration of the Rights of the Child on April 23, 1933 as depicted in this wall plaque in Kadıköy.

If Elgün were alive today she'd be lauded for her efforts and her story would be included in histories of remarkable women around the world. As it is, other than a biography written about her in Turkish, she's largely been overlooked. Only this plaque and a street bearing the name Nakiye Elgün on the other side of the city in Osmanbey exist to remind us of this powerhouse of a woman.

Address: Assuming you've come over to Kadıköy by boat from Eminönü, Kabataş or Karaköy, once you're on dry land orient yourself by turning so the water is behind you. To the left of you there's an open area where city buses depart from and a large square building on your right. Look straight ahead and you'll see a wide traffic filled road heading up a hill. That's Söğütlü Çeşme Caddesi. Cross over to the left-hand side of this road and walk along the covered pavement (about 130m) until you see the open area on your left. The relief is on the wall.

Şakirin Camii

Seen from the outside, Şakirin Camii looks like a space ship that's landed in the middle of a Turkish cemetery. Particularly when viewed at night. A patterned grill forming one of the exterior walls under the aluminium composite dome allows light to shine through from the inside. Two minarets and a square courtyard complete the form.

Şakirin Mosque is located in the Karacaahmet Mezarlığı, a very active cemetery a short bus ride from Kadıköy. It was commissioned by the Şakir brothers to commemorate their parents Semiha and İbrahim Şakir, who are buried in the cemetery. It opened on 7 May 2009 and can accommodate 500 people in prayer. There are always a lot of services being conducted but if you get the chance, go inside. The rather stark exterior and overall simple design of the complex lead you to expect an interior in the same style but that's not the case. Once inside, particularly when viewed from the women's section (set above the main prayer hall with an unobstructed view) you get a clear picture of the scope of architect Zeynep Fadıllıoğlu's vision. Fadıllıoğlu is a Turkish architect with a passion for modernity combined with traditional Ottoman design features. Both her grandfathers were in the textile business and she began collecting art as a teenager, before going onto study the history of art and design in London.

Fadıllıoğlu's personal beliefs and family history are woven into Şakirin so its impact comes through a composition that focuses on attention to detail, rather than grandeur and size. The interior is full of delicate textural motifs articulated in gold and green at ground level, and deep rich blues and salmon pinks up towards the dome. Glass teardrops hang from the chandelier, the dome is cast with scales and the mihrab takes inspiration from Rumi. The ornamentation is cleverly done so as not to overwhelm the senses. With three walls made from glass, the prayer space is open and light with shadows playing across and through juxtaposed screens and polished surfaces, creating a gentle river of movement across the floor. After sitting for a while and taking it all in I felt as though I was being safely cradled within a serenely beating heart.

Of note is the fact Fadıllıoğlu ended up with this commission by chance, after the male architect tasked with the job resigned before finishing it. She applied her considerable talents to create a truly 21st century place of worship, and is the first woman ever to design a mosque in Turkey.

Address: Nuhkuyusu Caddesi No 2, Üsküdar

You can catch any number of buses to the mosque from Kadıköy transport hub B. Take a 13, 14, 14F, 14R, 14Y or 15F and alight at the Zeynep Kamil Hastanesi bus stop. The mosque is just inside the entrance to the cemetery.

Şeyh Haydar Buhârî Türbesi

You come across many unusual features in Istanbul but one of my favourites and far and away the quirkiest are tombs dedicated to *dede*. Dede are senior dervishes most often associated with the Sufi religious orders such as the Mevlevi or Whirling Dervishes as they are known to tourists, and the lesser known Nakşibendis and Bektaşi dervish groups. Almost all of them trace their origins back to specific Muslim saints and teachers and take vows of poverty and austerity. It's not the aesthetics that make these tombs stand out, but their locations. Traffic has to drive around one dedicated to Gül Baba in the middle of a busy road in Merdivenköy, they take up space in the gardens of apartment buildings and even turn up at railway stations, as in the case of this one.

Buharalı Haydar Dede to give his full name, generally known as Haydar Baba, was the head or sheik of a Nakşibendi lodge, and is believed to have died around 1700 AD. He was buried in a traditional pale mint green tomb in a patch of land in Chalcedon. Chalcedon is the ancient name for modern day Kadıköy and Haydar Baba's tomb is now smack bang in the middle of the train lines leading to and from Haydarpaşa Railway Station. I can hear you thinking how impractical that must be (it is) and wondering why no one thought to move him. The reason is, no matter how inconvenient the location, Turkish people believe it's bad luck to move dervish tombs.

The Anatolian Railway company started work on Haydarpaşa, the terminus for the Baghdad and Hedjaz railways, in 1909. Two German architects, Otto Ritter and Helmut Conu, were hired to design the new building. Along with choosing a Neo-classical design for the structure and bringing over German and Italian stonemasons to chisel the embellishments, they decided the tomb would have to be moved. Plans were drawn up to lay the tracks and a time frame set. However rumour has it the night before work was due to start the supervisor of the works had a dream. Haydar Baba appeared and said it would make him uncomfortable if they moved his grave.

Shaken but undeterred the supervisor shrugged off his unease and went back to work the next day. The following night Haydar Baba came to the supervisor again and repeated his statement more forcefully this time, placing his hands around the man's throat and squeezing tightly. Seriously scared, the supervisor called a halt to the work and had the new lines laid on either side of the tomb, leaving Haydar Baba undisturbed.

Address: Entry off Haydarpaşa Garı Yolu, Kadıköy

When I first saw the tomb, Haydar Baba was at rest under a shady tree. The green metal fence protecting his tomb needed a lick of paint, but the plants were regularly watered and any fallen leaves picked up off the ground. It was surrounded by ongoing restoration works on the station and archaeological excavations in, under and around the site of the railway lines. Access depended on how much construction there was on the day you visited, and whether or not the security guards would let you in. Excavation works are ongoing and at the time of publication Haydar Baba was getting a new tomb.

Judging by the size of the structure, when it's finished I expect there will be regular opening hours.

Until that time, starting from the ferry wharf in Kadıköy, walk along Rıhtım Caddesi, the waterfront road, in the direction of Haydarpaşa Railway Station. At the end, past the dolmuş terminal, you come to a road bridge leading up the hill away from the water. You can see the tomb from the left-hand side and also get a good view of the dig taking place in Haydarpaşa Meadows, the previous name of the area where the railway platforms and lines were laid. Some of the most significant finds to date are a mausoleum from somewhere between the 4th and 3rd centuries BC, a section of Byzantine Sainte Bassa Church and a WWII bunker. The road also takes you to the turn off to Haydarpaşa İngiliz Mezarlığı (page 54) so you could combine both places in one outing.

Surp Takavor Ermeni Kilisesi

Over the years a lot of Kadıköy's history has been lost to fires, earthquakes and redevelopment. What remains is either still being unearthed over at the archaeological dig where the railway lines were laid to Haydarpaşa Railway Station or hidden by high walls. You'll find the Armenian Church of Surp Takavor behind one of them.

The present building dates to 1858 but Sarkis Hovhannesya, a teacher and historian, mentions a church on this site in his book *Osmanlı Tarihi*, Ottoman History, printed in 1771. He dates it to

72

1720 and describes it as a ruin. Other sources date the earlier church building to 1722 but say nothing about its condition. Named Surp Asdvadzadzin or Holy Mother of God church, it contained a chapel dedicated to Surp Takavor, Saint Takavor. The structure underwent major reconstruction in 1814 and reopened for worship on July 4 under the auspices of Abraham I, the Patriarch at the time. Just over a quarter of a century later the wooden church sustained damage due to an earthquake, and then burned down in 1855. A new brick church arose from the ashes under the reign of Patriarch Hagopos III with the help of the Erzerum Hacı Garabed Ağa Muradyan charity. Murat Garabetyan, the founder of the charity, was buried in the courtyard of the church on his death in 1862.

When the church reopened in 1858 it was commemorated with the new name Surp Takavor Kilisesi, or Christ the King Armenian Church. Two schools were opened in the same year in what is now the courtyard, but they have long since closed down. Throughout the 20th and early 21st centuries, several notable church-run charities expanded the courtyard, and enclosed the space between the cut stone entry facade of the church and the separate wooden Gothic style bell tower, with a glass paned wooden framed antechamber.

The church was designed using a closed cross floor plan rather than the open plan more common to Armenian church architecture. The middle section is capped by a high rimmed dome while the arms, the transepts, are under tiled roofs. Seen from a pew at the rear, the altar is the focus of attention. A painting of the baby Jesus in the arms of Mother Mary takes centre stage, beneath a semi dome painted a luminous blue, suggesting the heavens above. Delicate polycandelon, lights suspended from a triangle composed of three chains, hang from the walls next to large, bright chandeliers. The plain cream walls are adorned with religious paintings in rich oils and there are two oval shaped stained glass windows set one above the other on opposite walls.

The church is usually closed every day except Sundays, when you are more than welcome to observe and attend services. At other times you can enter the courtyard and look over the graves and enter the glass antechapel furnished with paintings and icons.

Address: Mukadderhane Caddesi No 44-1, Kadıköy

If you've come over to Kadıköy by boat from Eminönü, Kabataş or Karaköy, once you've disembarked stand so the water is behind you. Straight ahead you'll see a wide traffic filled street going up a hill. That's Söğütlü Çeşme Caddesi. Cross over so you're walking on the right-hand side of this street and turn right at Mühürdar Caddesi. Surp Takvor Ermeni Kilisesi is two blocks in.

Zühtü Paşa Camii

Like many neighbourhoods on the Asian side of Istanbul, Kızıltoprak was once full of old wooden houses inhabited by well off Turkish families. Scent laden rambling roses adorned high stone walls and ornately worked metal gates that opened onto green garden oases while shielding private lives from prying eyes. These days little remains of idyllic scenes such as these, except for Zühtü Paşa Camii. Situated on one of Istanbul's very many busy roads, Zühtü Paşa contains the largest number of examples of Kūfic writings of any mosque in Istanbul.

Kūfic writing is a type of handwritten Islamic script, believed to have first been used to record quotes from the Koran in the early Islamic centre of Kūfah, Iraq. The earliest existing copies of the Koran dating to the 8th century use a simple form of kufic script and later styles included floral, foliate, plaited, interlaced and other versions of kūfi.

The mosque was built between 1883 and 1884 on the order of Ahmed Zühtü Paşa (1833-1902), a statesman during the reign of Sultan Abdulhamid II (1876-1909). Abdülhamid II was a great fan of the Kūfic style of calligraphy and Armenian Krikor Köçeoğlu, also known as Krikor Köçeyan, was a master. His is the hand behind the constrained riot of colours created by the inscriptions of the Koran adorning the internal walls of this mosque. Recognised as the first non-Muslim calligraphy specialist in the Ottoman Empire, Köçeoğlu was born in the Kadıköy district but went to the Pangaltı Armenian School on the other side of the Bosphorus. Once there his talent was recognised, and later on his family sent him to study art at the Ecole Muradian in Paris. On his return to Istanbul

Köçeoğlu honed his skills, creating a unique style that combines Persian and Ottoman Kūfi.

Ahmed Zühtü Paşa greatly appreciated Köçeoğlu's artistry so commissioned him to decorate the interior of the mosque. Zühtü Paşa had worked his way through various ministerial positions in finance until he was appointed vizier, a high ranking official in the Ottoman Empire in the late 1880s. At the turn of the century his career took a turn when he moved to the Ministry of Education. In a short period of time he founded a primary school offering education free of charge. He used monies earned through real estate and land to fund the salaries of teachers and school employees, as well as cover the expense of running the mosque. The school operated from 1888 to 1921. At the same time Zühtü Paşa was thinking about, planning and researching education systems in various European countries, culminating in opening a *darülfünun*, a university, on August 19, 1900. He contributed greatly to education in Turkey and on top of all that, he was also a poet. On his death on April 12, in 1902, Ahmed was buried in the courtyard as stipulated in his will.

All this history becomes inconsequential once you're actually standing inside the mosque. I took advantage of my sex and headed to the women's section upstairs. It affords a great view of the interior and a quiet area to reflect on the art, design and culture embellishing the walls. On the day I visited the only people I saw inside were local shop owners and tradesmen. Lucky them I thought, it's such a beautiful place to worship or just sit and let the urgency of the outside world slowly slip away.

Address: Camii Sokak No15, Zühtüpaşa, Kadıköy

The easiest way to visit is to catch a 16D, FB2 or GZ1 from Kadıköy transport hub A and get off at the Kızıltoprak stop. Then you have to walk about a minute more in the same direction until you come to a pedestrian crossing at the traffic lights. The mosque is opposite. To return stay on the same side of the road as the mosque and walk back down Bagdat Caddesi until you reach the bus stop. Catch any bus marked Kadıköy.

ÜSKÜDAR AND SURROUNDING NEIGHBOURHOODS

Abdülmecit Efendi Köşk

Abdülmecit Efendi Köşk entry hall

The Abdülmecit Pavilion was built between 1880 and 1885 as a hunting lodge for Ismail Paşa, a former Khedive of Egypt (see Hıdıv Kasrı entry on page 104 for more information about the role of a khedive). Construction cost 20,000 Egyptian pounds with a further 8,000 spent on furnishings. Initially it was the only building in 50 acres of woodland in Nakkastepe. Later on additional structures were built including a *harem* for the women, a *selamlık* for the men and auxiliary buildings. Eventually it was appropriated by Abdüdulhamid II for the use of his uncle Abdülmecid Efendi. Now only the pavilion remains and it's owned by Ömer Koç. This Turkish businessman is an art collector and the chairman of Koç Holding AŞ, originally a family run business founded in 1926.

The köşk is used for contemporary art exhibitions, many of them both childlike and challenging. It sits nestled among mature trees and looks as though someone has put together a larger-than-life size gingerbread house, with swathes of decorative icing piped onto each panel. Each partition is the same size as the windows, resulting in a geometrically partitioned façade. Deep wide eaves and hand-carved decorations complete the look of something out of a fairy tale. The feeling of entering into an unknown land continues inside. The entryway opens onto a large *iwan*, a rectangular hall covered in tiles with a fountain at floor level. A fresco entitled *The Fountain of Love* by well-known Turkish painter Hüseyin Avni Lifij adorns a wall in one of the halls and every surface, be it a ceramic corner stove, recess or ceiling cornice, is covered in decorative allsorts. There are tiles in different colours, contrasting painted boiserie and simple wainscoting yet the overall look is elegantly muted. Each room works well as a gallery space. You never know what might be waiting through the next doorway, humans sculpted in a corner huddle or a giraffe lurching towards at you. Depending on the objects on display the lush grounds are sometimes incorporated into the exhibition design too.

Address: Kuşbakışı Caddesi No 18, Altunizade/Nakkastepe

This is one of the few places I suggest travelling to by bus as alternative options require too many changes of transport and instructions. From the waterfront at Kadıköy transport hub B take a 14M or 15F and get off at Icadiye Stop. The entry to the köşk is about 25 metres along from there, on the right.

Opening times: The pavilion is open whenever there is an exhibition. Entry is free and permitted between 11.00 and 19.00 every day except Mondays. Ask your hotel or accommodation host if there's an exhibition on when you come to Istanbul. You don't have to like modern art to appreciate the Abdülmecit Efendi Köşk but I think you'll probably warm to it in such a glorious setting.

Aziz Mahmud Hüdayî Türbesi

Be warned. Unless you have your own car or take a taxi, the Aziz Mahmud Hüdayî Tomb is up a hill. A very steep one. The day I went it was mid-summer which in Istanbul means stinking hot and humid. As anyone who knows the area will tell you, everywhere in Üsküdar is hilly, but luckily for me the ascent was short and sharp. As the tomb isn't too far up I made it without melting. Just.

Aziz (that's saint in Turkish) Mahmut Hüdayî lived from 1541 to 1628. His tomb is the second most visited religious site in Istanbul after Eyup Sultan Mosque on the Golden Horn, because Hüdayî was one of the most important sufi mystics of the Ottoman Empire. Along with Yahya Efendi, Telli

Baba and Hazreti Yuşa (the prophet Joshua), he is considered one of the four patron saints of the Bosphorus.

Hüdayî was an inspired poet, composer, Islamic scholar and writer, among other things. During his illustrious career he was in charge of the Küçuk Aya Sofya Camii, the little Hagia Sophia mosque, and preached in Fatih Mosque as well. Born in Sereflikoçhisar, Hüdayî died in Üsküdar and was laid to rest here, next to the mosque named for him.

His tomb is located in the Aziz Mahmud Hüdayî Külliyesi run by the Aziz Mahmud Hüdayî Foundation, a religious charity that also runs schools, a soup kitchen and student dormitories. The complex was established in 1589 when Hüdayî bought the land and had a dervish lodge built. More buildings were added in the following years and around 1598 the lodge was converted into a mosque. Many of the original structures were wooden and haven't survived, but those remaining are built into a slope so they're at odd angles to one another, casting interesting shadows at different times of the day. There's the mosque, various halls and administrative buildings, rose gardens, water fountains, small cemetery plots and of course Hüdayî's last resting place. His wooden tomb is located under a central dome held in place by four marble columns. It's painted the deep green of Islam and draped in a calligraphy embroidered heavy green velvet cloth. Gilded ironwork encloses it and hand drawn decorations cover the facades of the room. In death as in life Hüdayî is surrounded by his children and grandchildren, lying together in peace in tombs also covered in green cloth.

As is the case to enter a mosque, men and women are required to dress modestly and women need to cover their hair. Entry is via a small door leading into a glass vestibule built in 1912 by Princess Fatma Hanım, a daughter of the Egyptian Khedive Ismail Paşa. Leave your shoes in one of the pigeon holes provided and follow the people heading for the saint's tomb. Although it's a site of religious pilgrimage and people kneel or stand in prayer in front of the tomb, hands cupped and facing upwards, quietly reciting from the Koran, it's quite usual to see family groups sitting together on the carpet, small children lying by their side. However on the busiest days, Fridays and weekends, a security guard clad in fetching plaid slippers instructs people to keep moving along to make room for the endless stream of worshippers.

On my exit I noticed a man sitting at a desk covered in what looked like tickets but are receipts given to people who make cash donations. In addition to the other services they provide, the foundation organises culture symposiums, outings and entertainment for adults and children, and provides financial and other assistance through fundraising fairs and food donations.

When you leave the tomb take the short flight of stairs up to the next level. The mosque is on the left while the entry to the women's section, the wooden arch overhead, is on the right. I chose not to enter the mosque itself after hearing a man ask a young Turkish woman why she had entered the main section. She explained she wanted to take some photos and although their conversation was friendly enough I didn't want to intrude. I simply stood at the doorway and took in the pretty paintwork on what would otherwise be a rather plain wooden interior. The simplicity of the architecture is due to the structure starting out as a dervish lodge, while the decorations date to the reign of Sultan Abdülmecid in the 19th century, and reflect the fashions of the time.

The more elaborate of them are on the ceiling, and I was able to see them up close from the women's section. The entrance to this section is across from the mosque, up two flights of stairs leading to the interior of the wooden arch you see stretching above the courtyard as you approach the tomb. The rooms are small with low ceilings and usually full of women praying or reading the Koran. Lattices shield women from being seen by those in the mosque interior below but still allow you to admire the floral designs on the cornices and panelled painted ceiling. They look almost French in style.

The people I encountered in the complex were very friendly and happy for me to take photographs. It helps that I speak Turkish but I've always found good intentions are rewarded in Turkey, and my interest in the culture and traditions delights most people I meet. Do note, I always ask permission to take photos of places or individuals and operate by the maxim, if in doubt, don't.

Address: Aziz Mahmut Efendi Sokak No 9, Aziz Mahmut Hüdayi, Üsküdar

The easiest way to get there is to walk along Hakimiyeti Milliye Caddesi. That's the main street leading from the waterside Üsküdar Meydanı. It's fairly flat until you come to Tepsi Fırını Sokak which is where you turn right and head upwards and upwards. When you get to the T-intersection there's a simple wooden building on the right-hand corner. It's the tomb of Hazreti Cennet Mehmet Efendi, a saint who died in the 17th century. The interior is a bit plain but it's worth stopping to peer in through the windows at this enclosed cemetery. When you're done continue along to the entry of the complex on the left-hand side of the street.

Opening times: 09.00-18.00, Tue–Sun. Closed Mondays.

Milli Saraylar Beykoz Cam ve Billur Müzesi

The Beykoz Crystal and Glass Museum is housed in former stables on land once owned by Abraham Paşa, the *kethüda* or chief steward of Ismail Paşa, the Khedive of Egypt. Abraham Paşa eventually rose in rank to become the vizier of Sultan Abdülaziz. Looking more like a large country house, today the stable buildings stand alone in a large wooded grove but when they were built there were also pavilions, ornamental pools, a theatre and aviaries in the grounds. The approach to the museum is through a large grassed area ringed by tall mature trees. Even through there's a highway just on the other side you don't really notice it on account of the greenery all around you. Many of the plants and flowers aren't native to Turkey. Abraham Paşa had them brought into the country to plant in his gardens, including 117 different species of tree. A kids' playground and outdoor cafe complete the picture.

The museum takes its name from the Beykoz Cam ve Billurât Fabrika-i Hümayunu, the Beykoz Imperial Glass and Crystal Factory, established during the reign of Sultan Abdülmecid in 1846. The 19th century was a period of intense industrialisation in Turkey and the Beykoz area was chosen as an industrial zone.

Once you've donned your galoshes at the entry door and shown your ticket, take advantage of the free audio guides on offer. I'm not usually a big fan of them but the hand pieces are light and easy to use and the English explanations are clear and not too overburdened with facts. Basically you'll hear what's written on the information panels but with additional information about the videos and the artefacts on display. There are a lot of them, 1,500 to be precise, dating from the Anatolian Selçuk era in the 13th century through to the 19th century, towards the end of Ottoman rule.

The history of glass making in Turkey is well explained in the information panels. It's useful for history buffs but I came for the glass. The Selçuk era is represented by opalescent fragments of glass from the 13th century, and sacred and secular

85

examples of Memluk oil lamps. The former are inscribed with *sülüs,* a style of Arabic script, while the latter dance with birds chittering in brilliant foliage. The curators have also cleverly animated miniatures from the time, showing glass makers producing or displaying their wares. They're projected up on screens alongside actual tools and examples from the period shown in the art work. The most important of the early pieces is a Kubadabad plate, dating from 1237 to 1246 AD, made using a free blowing technique. It was found during excavation of the site of a palace of the same name, near Lake Beyşehir in the Konya region. Although broken it is almost complete and decorated with sophisticated enamel and gilding.

There's a fabulous room full of *revzenler.* These are the coloured glass windows you often see in mosques and tombs, set above eye level, allowing light to enter. They add movement and colour to the overall design. Here they're back lit so the patterns they make are refracted onto the floor. Have a look at the simple one made by framing round panes of opaque white glass directly opposite the entrance. It was made by Mimar Sinan. Mimar Sinan is considered the greatest of all Ottoman architects and was commissioned to build mosques and a variety of structures by Sultan Süleyman (Süleyman the Magnificent) and other Ottoman leaders.

Huge glass demijohns covered in wicker, used to store spring water for drinking are displayed along one wall, interspersed with *karlık.* These glass containers have an inner glass compartment nesting inside them to form a narrow space for *kar,* snow, and were used to keep food cool. I love them for their simple clean lines but was equally impressed by the more ornate items on display in the museum.

The Turkish selections include Venetian produced lamps made to order for Grand Vizier Mehmet Sokullu Paşa in 1569, *laledanlar,* vases made to hold a single flower that became fashionable in Europe during the tulip craze and of course *çeşme bülbül. Eye of the Nightingale* as it is known in English, is made from lining up thin rods of coloured glass next to one another then heating them to high temperatures so they become bound together without the individual colours melting into one another. The first piece of *çeşme bülbül* was created in 1847 using alternating rods of clear and blue glass. The blue and clear twist pattern is the most well-known and the museum has several cabinets of it from tiny vials women used to dab on perfume to large presentation bottles and *zem zem* water sets, used to dispense holy water brought back from pilgrimage to Mecca. Further on there are glistening vases in Aventurine glass, a form of quartz imitated in the examples on show and a section dedicated to calligraphy on glass. A reverse painted glass panel showing a seven-pointed star stood out to me.

Work from Europe includes Murano glassware, Moser of Bohemia and France represented by glassmakers Gallé and Daum. Osler from England makes an appearance but is really overshadowed by the house of Baccarat. There are 19th century Baccarat crystal sherbet dispensers, perfume bottles and powder boxes, bowls and plates. In another room there's a cabinet full of Vetro Filigranato, the candy cane stripe technique that originated in Italy on the island of Murano that migrated to Turkey to become çeşme bülbül. Look out for the cabinet with the ceramic gun. I thought it looked really odd and then a security guard told me it was a *gülabdan*, a perfume dispenser. It turns out novelty shaped gülabdan were all the rage in the 19th century.

Each time I entered a room I saw the most beautiful objects on display. Then I stepped into the next space and it was even more wonderful. By the time I reached the Cam Köşk, the Glass Pavilion, I'd run out of basic adjectives, moved through the superlatives and could do nothing but gawp in amazement, unable to find the right words to describe the splendour before me. The images, however, are clear in my mind. Taking photographs of the displays is not allowed, and the helpful guard I spoke with thanked me for following the rules, in between chasing down miscreants. I didn't mind the restriction. If it were allowed, I'd never get out.

The Glass Pavilion was the work of Englishman William James Smith in Dolmabahçe Palace for Sultan Abdülmedit. Designed as a viewing platform that allowed the sultan to look out onto the street, it took two years to complete from 1853 to 1854. All the crystal and glass fittings were brought from England and everything you see in the room, baring the reproduction fountain, is original. The creativity and whimsy employed are enchanting and it is hard to take it all in. A divine all glass bird cage with clear rods and ruby glass roof was one piece I particularly liked, but the floor lamps, one with a peacock with its tail picked out in illuminated glass, beads and semiprecious stones, took my breath away.

The next room has a veritable army of Baccaret glassware adorning a long table in a room that is extremely glamorous, but somewhat more muted than the one before. It's a good thing because it gives your senses a rest before you enter the last display space. Glass dressing screens and fire shields compete for attention with a glass upright piano and glass carriage, a la Cinderella, made for Sultan Mahmud II. The carriage is covered in harlequin pattern-coloured panes of glass on the outside and the interior is lined with mirrored panels.

If you want to visit the museum in the morning catch a number 15 from the Üsküdar Bosphorus bus terminal and get off at the Beykoz stop. You can catch a ferry from Üsküdar to Beykoz but the first one doesn't go until 11.45. The trip takes around 1 hour and 20 mins. From Beykoz you can walk up Şahinkaya Caddesi and then turn right into Mehmet Yavuz Caddesi and continue up the hill, past the Beykoz Korusu until you come to a small overhead bridge. Once you've walked under it you'll see the entry to the museum on your left, about 50 metres further on. However you choose to travel make time to stop at the İshak Ağa Çeşmesi. You'll pass it as you walk up Şahinkaya Street, before the turn off.

It's impossible to miss. If the walk sounds too much, there's a taxi stand next to the bus stop.

If you have time on the walk back down take a wander through the Beykoz Korusu on your left. It's one of the few former privately owned groves on either side of the Bosphorus still in existence. There's a council run restaurant called a Sosyal Tesisler in the grounds if you're hungry. When you're done head back to Beykoz and catch the ferry to Üsküdar. The last one leaves at 17.45. Having caught the bus back myself, I don't recommend it at all. The coast road is one lane either way with frequent bottlenecks as the day wears on. Even if you do manage to get a seat, it's an hour or more of your time better spent enjoying Istanbul's famous waterway.

Address: Mehmet Yavuz Caddesi No 115, Beykoz

Opening time: 09.00-17.00, Tue–Sun. Closed Mondays. Entrance cost 60tl.

Fethi Paşa Korusu

Once upon a time both sides of the Bosphorus were covered in forests, carefully tended gardens and wide-open fields, but over the centuries, particularly the most recent, these have been replaced by a sprawl of higgledy-piggledy apartment blocks, contemporary villas and gleaming, towering office blocks. Fortunately, here and there all along the shores, botanical reminders of the city's past remain. Fethi Paşa Korusu is one of them. The word *koru* means grove or small wood and during Ottoman times they were areas where hunting and the cutting down of trees were forbidden.

Tophane Müşiri Fethi Ahmet Paşa was an Ottoman governor, ambassador and minister. He was also known as Rodosizade, the son of Rodos, because his father Hafız Ahmet Ağa came from Rhodes. Fethi Ahmet was born on the Greek island in 1801. He married Atiye Sultan, the daughter of Sultan Mahmud II and half-sister of Sultans Abdülmecid I and Abdülaziz. During his term in office he was the first Ottoman ambassador to Vienna, attended the 1839 coronation ceremony of Queen Victoria of England and even met with the pope.

Spare a thought for him if you visit Hagia Eirene or the Istanbul Archaeological Museum. He's the one who changed the church from being a warehouse storing old weaponry into the very first museum exhibiting archaeological artefacts. He also initiated the archaeological excavations in Sultanahmet Square in 1847 and was behind the development of the Beykoz Glass Factory. It was under his watch that their Çeşm-i Bülbül, glassware featuring streaks of blue and white twisting around the form, became famous.

I'm now a fairly fit person but used to suffer badly from asthma. Living in such a hilly city where getting out and about often means traversing at times sheer vertical paths means I've become very strategic in how I approach certain places. Fethi Ahmet Paşa has two main entrances, one down by the water at Paşa Liman Park and the other a short easy walk from Fıstıkağaç Metro stop, on the metro line that runs from Üsküdar. I chose the latter. Once inside the woods a series of paths gently crisscross down the steep slope and as you descend all you can hear are the sounds of birds chirping. If you're lucky you might see a colourful kingfisher sitting in a tree. The trees are magnificent. There are pines of all types including a very rare Japanese velvet, species of oak, maple and horse chestnut, persimmon, locust, yew and ash. By the time you get to the bottom you'll have accrued your months' worth of oxygen through forest bathing and feel like you've just come back from a restorative break from the city.

It's remarkable, given that after Fethi Ahmet's death in Istanbul in 1858 his descendants basically abandoned the grove. In 1958 one of them, a lawyer named Şevket Mocan transferred his shares to the Istanbul Municipality Council. Over time the council acquired more of the land and managed it under the name Mocan Korusu. In 2003 they restored the two köşk now used as a cafe and a restaurant. They're part of the council owned and run Sosyal Tesisler, social facilities, serving traditional Turkish meals at reasonable prices, often in gorgeous locations and buildings like these. The canteen-like café with direct views over the water offers basic foods like wraps, hamburgers and *simit*, as well as a traditional Turkish breakfast. What makes it particularly appealing to me is the fact the large decking area covered in wisteria is completely non-smoking, and they mean it. There's a smaller area for smokers one floor up, if you must. You can enjoy a buffet breakfast there on weekends but go early.

Above the café, a larger köşk houses a restaurant with tables arranged on three separate terraces, all non-smoking. Köşk, summer pavilion, is a bit of a misnomer really as this imposing wooden house with lovely decorative features (make sure to visit the toilets, even if you don't need to go, just so you can see the interior) was home to Turkish writer and translator Cemil Meriç from 1946 to 1960. During his career he wrote about the social sciences, with twelve books to his name. If I lived somewhere like this, with staff to maintain it and me, I'm sure I could be equally productive.

Address: Fethi Paşa Korusu, Kuzguncuk, Üsküdar

Wherever you're staying in Istanbul, Üsküdar is the best starting point to visit the grove. If you want to follow my lead, catch the metro one stop up to Fıstıkağaç, then walk about 10 minutes to the entry in Münir Ertegün Sokak. Otherwise catch a bus from the Üsküdar Bosphorus bus terminal. Bus numbers 15, 15B, 15C, 15S and 15Y will take you the two stops to the park. Alight at the Paşalimanı bus stop and head up the path.

Opening times: Nilhan Sultan Köşkü Paşalimanı (cafe) 09.00-23.00, 7 days a week. Fethipaşa Sosyal Tesisleri (restaurant) 08.30-23.00, 7 days a week.

Hıdıv Kasrı

Istanbul has long been a divided city. Physically it's split by the Bosphorus Strait, a watery barrier stretching from the Black Sea to the Sea of Marmara. Under its surface are unpredictable fast-flowing currents only locals can safely navigate. Hundreds of years ago the city was also divided geopolitically. A diverse mix of Muslims, Christians and Jews, with allegiances both inside and outside the Ottoman Empire was overseen by the formal rules and exacting regulations of the imperial courts of the sultans. Life in Istanbul was anything but peaceful so rulers sought solutions and respite in *kasır*. Strictly speaking these were pavilions or summer palaces but in reality they were much more.

Hıdiv Kasrı, in Hıdiv Kasrı Korusu or grove, up on a hill in Beykoz, was one of them. Unlike others in the city that were built for Ottoman leaders, Hıdiv Kasrı was the residence of Khedive Abbas Hilmi II of Egypt and Sudan. A *khedive* represented the Ottoman Empire in Egypt, wielding power on their behalf. Abbas Hilmi II was the great-great-grandson of Muhammad Ali who ruled Egypt from 1805 to 1845. He is considered the founder of modern Egypt. Throughout his reign Muhammad Ali tried but ultimately failed to wrest control of his country from the British. Nonetheless he managed to set up independent income streams and production, which meant the Ottoman Empire's control over Egypt was only ever nominal.

When Abbas Hilmi II became khedive in 1892 he set out to realise Muhammad Ali's dream. Unlike his predecessors he thought the best course of action would be to woo the Ottomans into believing they would benefit from helping oust the British from Egypt and Sudan. A successful seduction requires the perfect setting, so with this in mind he employed the services of a famous architect to build Hıdiv Kasrı, or Çubuklu Vılla, as it's also known. Just which architect that was depends on what source you believe. Some suggest it is the work of Austro-Hungarian born architect Antonio Lasciac who made his name designing palaces in Egypt, assisted by Italian architect Delfo Seminati. Still others say it is from the hand of Italian Raimondo D'Aronco, the man behind Şeyh Zafir tomb (see page 129) and Botter Apartments on Istiklal Caddesi in Beyoğlu.

The khedive's second wife wrote in her memoir that she was instrumental in designing the layout of the structure with Lasciac and Seminati, and personally selected the wallpapers, upholstery materials and French and German furniture decorating the rooms. A countess, she was born May Torok von Szendro on June 15, 1877, in Philadelphia. After becoming involved with Abbas Hilmi II, she converted to Islam and took the Muslim name Zubeida bint Abdallah. She soon changed this, calling herself Princess Cavidan Hanim or simply Lady Djavidan. In her recollections she was also responsible for landscaping the palace gardens, right down to deciding how the footpaths would wind and where each tree would go. The Rose Garden was her especial favourite, as it was planted to commemorate their great love. It's best appreciated from the rooms on the first floor of the kasır.

Construction was completed in 1907 and Abbas Hilmi II moved in. Regardless of exactly who was responsible for the overall plan and individual details of Hıdiv Kasrı, the end result is unique. The ground floor rooms flow one into the other, with an indoor courtyard where water softly babbles in a marble fountain lit by a glass ceiling. This room opens out to a terrace around a pool. Gleaming Art Deco light fittings compete for attention with highly polished wood fittings in a curved dining room known as the Crystal Hall. A small elegant elevator, caged in an Art Nouveau brass frame glides slowly upwards. A few of the six rooms on the upper floor, used as bedrooms, are open to the public. Throughout the building windows offer glimpses of the Bosphorus amidst the swirling boughs of mature trees.

Cavidan Hanim didn't officially join Abbas Hilmi II in the kasır for another three years, in 1910, when they were formally married, but I can easily see her being the centre of attention at parties. I imagine her dazzling with her beauty and wit while her consort conversed with the officials he hoped would help gain Egypt's autonomy. It wasn't all smooth sailing though. According to one story the khedive liked to hoist his flag from the tower, offending the Turkish government located on the opposite shores of the Bosphorus at Yıldız Palace. Only official embassies were allowed to fly their country's flag, but Abbas Hilmi II persisted. Depending on current policy it's sometimes possible to enjoy the views from the top of the tower. Somehow I am sure this was something Abbas Hilmi II did a lot before his departure from the kasır in 1914. He was removed by the British ending his days known as the Khedive of Egypt and Sudan.

Address: Hıdiv Kasrı Caddesi/Koru Sokak, Hıdiv Kasrı Korusu, Beykoz

The Şehir Hat (City Line) ferry from Üsküdar to Çubuklu takes an hour and travels up the Asian side of the Bosphorus. It's about a 20-minute walk up hill to Hıdiv Kasrı. The hill is painfully steep so you might want to catch a taxi. There's a cafe and restaurant on the premises. Both are run by the council under the Beltur brand. No alcohol is served and prices are reasonable.

Opening times: As of the date of publication of this guide the interior of the kasır was closed for renovations. It's expected to open again later in 2023. Currently it's only possible to visit the grounds and the cafe, which operates 09.00-23.00, 7 days a week.

Marmara Üniversitesi İlahiyat Fakültesi Camii ve Kültür Merkezi

The blindingly white Marmara University Faculty of Theology Mosque sits on a vast expanse of equally brilliant tiling. When the sun hits the green coloured glass bricks inserted into the dome, the shape seems to ripple and undulate. Otherwise all is still, with only a *şadırvan*, an ablutions fountain and *musalla*, the stone rests coffins are placed on, visible at street level. Historically, mosques are situated in large courtyard complexes comprised of libraries, *medrese,* separate şadırvan for men and women, toilets and food kitchens.

The contemporary design and air of serenity created by the open space seems oddly incongruous with the cacophony of traffic passing alongside, the buses crowding around the stop in front of the shopping centre in the next block, and the mass of people heading off in all directions. However what you see from the outside is a small part of a whole complex designed to reflect the Islamic concept that civilisation is only as strong as its parts. Construction began in 2014 and was completed in 2016. The architects decided on a dodecagon, a 12-sided polygon shape for the centre of the mosque. It was created using 12 steel columns set above a reinforced concrete base and the diameter and height are both 35 metres.

This dome encases the interior space and was designed using the geometrical concept of fractals. In this concept, each part has the same statistical character as the total structure, like pattern forms in snowflakes. This reflects the place of the individual in Islam, where each person is a small part of a much larger unified community. The dome was handcrafted using a traditional carpentry method called *kırlıngıc*. In this dovetail technique the beams are joined using interlocking fan-tail shaped cut outs so each piece of the dome is complete in itself. All put together, as with fractals, the beams create a new and equally valuable whole. Rays of light enter through walls composed of lattice work concrete. The patterns they form on the carpet echo those that come from above.

Standing in the centre of this space feels like being held safely in a cocoon. Underground, directly below your feet, there are classrooms, a conference hall, exhibition spaces, a *mescit,* a small mosque or prayer room, a library, café and numerous tables and chairs for those wanting to sit and study or just chat. Inside the mosque a mathematically articulated universe swirls around you while the heavens beckon from above. The skylight at the very top, made from framed triangles of glass to form a honeycomb, is inspired by *mukarnas*. These are architectural devices built into half domes in more traditional mosques that provide support and act as transition points in a building's design. Mathematically the design has no boundaries. It can be as large or as small as the space allows, similar to the composition of fractals. Conceptually each embodies the Islamic ideals of fluidity and replication.

The abstract stylisations in the Marmara University Faculty of Theology Mosque reinterpret classical Ottoman style to create a modern, almost futuristic architectural language. Meaning is reduced to its micro and macro components, with each part making up the whole and the whole being found in each part.

Address: Mahir İz Caddesi No 2, Altunizade, Üsküdar

To explore this for yourself, you can catch any number of buses from the Üsküdar inland bus stop. The 11BE, 11C, 11P, 11ÜS or 12A all stop at the Marmara Üniversitesi İlahiyat Fakültesi stop, just before the Capitol AVM (Shopping Centre). Using the bus lets you see more of the area but they can be crowded and slow depending on the traffic. The metro from Üsküdar is a quicker option (make sure you don't confuse it with the Marmaray as they both have the same entrance point underground). The Bağlarbaşı metro stop is only two stops along the line and the mosque is directly above it.

Nevmekan Bağlarbaşı

I'm a fan and champion of public transport so when I found out, back in 2012, there was a transport museum a bus ride away from my home, naturally I went to see it. Located in Bağlarbaşı, up the hill from Üsküdar, it was in a marvellous building designed by Ali Talat Bey, a famous architect of the late Ottoman period. Talat Bey was one of the pioneers of Neo-classical Turkish architecture and a member of the First National Architecture Movement. The structure I saw then had been custom built for the IETT to function as the hangar and power station for the Üsküdar-Bağlarbaşı-Kısıklı tram line. Construction began in 1911, the later years of the Empire, but it was only completed in 1928 after the Republic was formed. Trams stopped running on the Asian side of Istanbul in

1966 and the building became a bus garage, closing in 1998. It then took on new life as a transport museum.

I was thrilled to see restored horse drawn trams as well as examples of the first electric models still with their destinations inscribed in Ottoman Turkish cursive, inside the cavernous space. Large glass windows, their individual panes framed in thin strips of metal let in swathes of light. From the outside I could see the arches were slightly pointed in a nod to Selçuk architectural styles and a lone tower was topped with a pointed metal roof. The rest of the interior was largely bare, as befitting a former depot.

However a space this wonderful deserved to be shared and in 2016 it opened as the beautifully restored and repurposed Nevmekan Bağlarbaşı. Nevmekan is the combination of two words, *nev* meaning new in Farsi and *mekan* meaning place or venue. This 'new place' was the start of a government initiative to create what they refer to as Millet Kıraathanesi. In Turkish, *millet* means folk or people and *kıraathane*, derived from Arabic, means reading house. There are kıraathane all over Turkey. Traditionally they are male domains where men meet to chat, read the papers and play cards, *tavla* (backgammon) or *Okey* (a game using tiles in which players compete to score the most points). Tea drinking is major part of their activities even though these establishments are commonly referred to as coffee houses.

Nevmekan Bağlarbaşı is essentially a people's cafe that combines a multi-purpose library, study space, art gallery and cafe, open to all. The interior has been designed along Ottoman luxury aesthetics with the metal beams painted in rich reds, plush velvet seating upholstered in jewel-like colours and sparking chandeliers reminiscent of *cami avizesi*, the metal hoops ringed with lights suspended below the main dome in the centre of mosques. The original upper balconies have been converted into cosy study nooks, with work tables and even a grand piano. If you're lucky someone will sit down to play it while you're there. Shelves of books take up the ground floor which leads to a pretty plant-filled garden out the back, The art gallery is in the basement.

Address: Gazi Caddesi No 12, Üsküdar

The simplest way to visit is by bus from the Üsküdar inland bus stop. Catch an 11ÜS, 11Y or 12A and alight at Bağlarbaşı Kültür Merkezi. I suggest you screenshot the 3-minute walk from the bus stop to Nevmekan for reference. Depending on your schedule you might want to stay for lunch or a treat. The cafe is run by the council so the prices are reasonable and the atmosphere is very relaxing. When you're done you can return the same way. Alternately continue down Gazi Caddesi to Üsküdar. This street takes you through traditional neighbourhoods and comes out in the middle of Üsküdar Çarşı, the neighbourhood's lively and interesting shopping area. It's only a few blocks back from the water where the buses, trains and ferries are located.

Opening times: 08.00-23.00, 7 days a week

Nevmekan Sahil

University students around the world face a lot of the same challenges, one of which is the need to find quiet areas where they can study. This isn't always easy, especially when they only have a small budget like many of the university students who come from cities, towns and villages all across Turkey to study in Istanbul. A large number live in student dormitories where they share rooms with up to seven other people or in crowded share houses so space and silence are limited.

This makes Nevmekan Sahil on the Üsküdar waterfront a favourite venue of theirs. Like Nevmekan Bağlarbaşı, Nevmekan Sahil was conceived as a millet kıraathanesi. It was built to enlarge the 60,000 strong collection of books in the library across the road in the Şemsi Paşa Camii, and holds more than 100,000 books. On the main floor there are quiet areas for study, a cafe space with a stage used for musical performances and book readings, meeting rooms and daycare area. The library collection continues downstairs where there's an art gallery that's shown works by world famous photographer Ara Güler, *ebru* expert Hikmet Barutçigil and numerous foreign artists.

The architects behind Nevmekan Sahil are Hassas Mimarlik, the same team who created the Marmara Üniversitesi İlahiyat Fakültesi Camii ve Kültür

Merkezi in Altunizade. From the outside Nevmekan Sahil looks like a conventional building. Apart from stripes picked out in an orange red colour along the facing, there's nothing particularly remarkable about it. Or so it seems. Once you pass through security head directly for the main hall and look up. The interior is breathtaking, not a word I often use.

Instead of a traditional ceiling, the roof was constructed by sitting sixteen wooden beams on a hexagonal frame, to create a lattice shell in fractal. Basically it looks like a geometric chrysanthemum with enormous petals opening out over the space below. The architects employed engineering techniques common in Islamic architecture, such as double-centred arches in a dome form to suggest movement and express the idea that life in Islam is conceived as being two-fold. It revolves around the axis of the world we live in now and the hereafter. A frieze showing old Istanbul wraps all the way around the circular base, above shelves of books waiting to be read. I like to time my visits for lunch. Although the food on the menu isn't anything out of the ordinary it's well-priced and I get to sit in this gorgeous space and just soak it all in. Before leaving I check the latest offerings in the art gallery. More often than not it's something I want to see.

On sunny days I take a turn in the small but well manicured courtyard out the back. It's designated smoke free which makes for a refreshing change in Istanbul. You'll also find the Üsküdar Hanım Sultanlar Müzesi there. You can read about it on page 119.

The Nevmekan Sahil building replaced the old council owned Üsküdar marriage registry building

The ceiling/roof of Nevmekan Sahil

that suffered fire damage in 2012 before being sold to a private foreign owner in 2013. Turkish media widely reported a world class hotel was to be built in its place, but that never eventuated. The next news announcements pertained to the opening of Nevmekan Sahil on 3 October 2018. Just how the plot came to be in the possession of the municipality once more is unclear, but not knowing does nothing to detract from the beauty contained withing the building.

Address: Şemsi Paşa Caddesi No 2, Üsküdar

Nevmekan Sahil is a 5-minute walk from Üsküdar Meydanı, the large open square by the water, in the direction of Kız Kalesi, the Maiden's Tower, built on a rock out in the Bosphorus.

Opening times: 09.00-23.00, cafe and restaurant, 7
days a week
08.00-23.00, library, 7 days a week

Şemsi Paşa Camii

From the land, the single minaret of the Şemsi Paşa Camii right on the water's edge in Üsküdar appears twinned with the Boğaz Trafik Sinyalizasyon Kulesi (Bosphorus Traffic Signal Tower). However the mosque predates the shipping traffic control tower by some 420 years. It was designed by Mimar Sinan in 1580 at the request of one Şemsi Ahmet Paşa, a member of the Isfendiyar family. Şemsi Paşa served as a vizier to three Ottoman sultans, including Süleyman the Magnificent.

The design of the mosque is very simple, consisting of a single large dome sitting on an octagonal drum. The minaret only has one balcony with few embellishments and the building is angled away from the water, protecting the entryway from the sometimes buffeting gales. Now there is an *alem*, a traditional crescent on top of the dome, but originally there was a gilded sun said to represent the man for whom it's named, Şemsi, meaning solar or sun. Inside there's a piece of cloth in a picture frame set high on the wall. It's from the Kaaba in Mecca. The vast cloth covering the holy stone is changed every year and pieces of the old one distributed as much revered gifts. Small marble columns set on either side of the *mihrab*, the prayer niche, are used to test whether the building has been damaged after an earthquake. If they can't be turned it means the foundations have moved.

Şemsi's tomb is in a room built onto one side of the structure, designed to be viewed through an iron grill from the inside of the mosque itself. On my most recent visit it was covered by a curtain and the main interior had been altered with the addition of screens partitioning off a separate prayer space for women. There are mausoleums and other tombstones in a side garden, and twelve *medrese* rooms that were converted and opened as a public library on 29 May, 1953, the 500th anniversary of the conquest of Istanbul.

On my first visit some years ago I had the pleasure of being shown around by Turkish war veterans who'd fought in Korea during the Cold War. They told me tales full of sadness and bravery before going back to their favourite spot in the courtyard to take in the sun. Şemsi Paşa is a small mosque but it's jam-packed with history and fascinating stories. My favourite is the one about its nickname, Kuşkonmaz Camii, meaning the mosque on which birds do not land. Legend has it the name comes from the belief birds don't stand or build nests on the mosque as a sign of respect. I much prefer this version to the more mundane logic that points out the strong crosswinds blowing off the Bosphorus make it impossible for them to alight on the dome.

Address: Mimarsinan Mahallesi, Üsküdar

The mosque is an easy stroll from Üsküdar Meydanı, the open square at the waterfront, next to the ferry wharves and opposite the Marmaray Station.

Opening times for Şemsi Paşa's tomb: 08.30-17.00, Tue-Sun. Closed Mondays.

Üsküdar Hanım Sultanlar Müzesi

The Sultana Doll Museum in a building in the garden of Nevmekan Sahil museum showcases exquisitely perfect miniature dolls clad in typical outfits worn by men and women from the upper echelons of Ottoman society. One side of the room is dedicated to replicas of real-life Ottoman Sultans and the other to the Sultanas. Descriptions in the museum make much of the role royal women played in the development of society, with mention of their contributions in the form of mosques, hamam, fountains, covered bazaars and various charitable foundations. You don't need to like clothes to appreciate the exhibition but lovers of historical Turkish miniseries, like Mühteşem Yüzyıl, will be in seventh heaven.

An academic research committee spent months developing, drawing and completing final design boards for each doll, worthy of an exhibition in their own right. They examined original garments from the Ottoman harem of the 16th to the 19th century the sewer in me would love to see up close, to identify and determine the materials used. Eight specialists then worked for two months to custom make the

Lady Sultan Hanzade

outfits, replicating exactly the type of cloths used, the embellishments, whether applique or tiny embroidery stitches, right down to the smallest details including the placement of jewellery in headpieces and on the shoes. The ornamentation runs the gamut of plush furs, bulbous faux pearls and shiny sapphires, moulded leather collars, rich brocades, whisper thin silks, in colours as bright as a rainbow or as muted as a field of wheat after heavy rains.

Calling them dolls does them an injustice. Each figure was painstaking hand fashioned using tragacanth, a natural white gum, and their features faithfully reproduced according to existing paintings and miniatures of the individual in question. The finished result is a collection of uniquely different personalities, clad in outfits befitting their position in the Ottoman court, their official duties and personal traits.

Address: Şemsi Paşa Caddesi No 2, Nevmekan Sahil, Üsküdar

Nevmakan Sahil is a 5-minute walk from Üsküdar Meydanı, the large open square by the water. If the weather's nice I like to dawdle, check out how the people fishing along the edge of the Bosphorus are doing and just stop and gaze, mesmerised by the fast running current. It's even better on a windy day, or when it's snowing.

Opening time: 10.00-17.00, Tue-Sun. Closed Mondays. Free entry.

Validebağ Korusu

Planes to Istanbul fly over a staggering number of breeze block apartment buildings on their journey to the runway at the new airport. It, like the city, appears supersized, which is to be expected in a place with a population of over 15 million residents and counting. That's only the official figure. Most days it feels like a lot more.

Green spaces are few and far between, so even the smallest postage stamp size of greenery is highly valued. Luckily some of them are quite big, such as Validebağ Korusu, the second largest green area on the Anatolian side of Istanbul. It covers an area of 354,000 m² and has a long and unusual history starting sometime in the 18th century. That's when Mihrişah Valide Sultan, the mother of Sultan Selim III who ruled from 7 April 1789 to 29 May 1807, wanted to take advantage of the rolling hills and groves of trees in what is now the modern-day district of Çamlica. Ever willing to please his mum, Sultan Selim arranged for a small house to be built for her, surrounded by fields of grape vines. Some years later ownership of the land was transferred to Sultan Abdülmecid I who ruled from 1 July 1839 to 25 June 1861. Abdülmecid gave it to his mother Bezmialem Valide Sultan as a gift. It was named Validebağ after Bezmialem decided to create a botanical garden using her position and contacts to obtain tree and plant species from Turkey and all over the world.

After her death in 1853 the land passed into the hands of the Altunizade family. Altunizade Ismail Zühtü Paşa had a wonderful *köşk* built in the grounds and the reigning sultan of the time, Abdülaziz, was so moved by the elaborate pavilion that Zühtü Paşa gave it to him. Sultan Abdülaziz also built his own hunting lodge nearby but when people continued to refer to the köşk as Ismail Paşa Konağı, Ismail Paşa's mansion, Abdülaziz had it demolished. He engaged the services of Ottoman court architect Nigoğos Balyan to build a summer pavilion on the grounds in its place, and presented it to his mother Pertevniyal Valide Sultan. On her death in 1883 it passed to Adile Sultan.

Adile Sultan was the half sister of both Sultan Abdülmecid I and Sultan Abdülaziz. The latter ruled the Empire from 25 June 1861 to 30 May 1876 and the two men were half brothers. Adile Sultan established her own charitable foundation and was active in education and social welfare. While her husband Mehmet Ali Paşa enjoyed the Abdülaziz Hunting Lodge, she used the former summer pavilion as a divan, an office similar to a council of state where people could come to her with requests for assistance. Adile Sultan was the only woman in the history of the Empire to have her own divan.

After her death in 1899 the building served many purposes. In the early years of the Turkish Republic the Adile Sultan Pavilion was converted into a 60-bed home for the orphaned children of soldiers who died in battle, where they could convalesce from tuberculosis. It expanded further to become a sanatorium in 1939 and operated as such until 1957 when it was handed over to the Department of Education and ran as a teaching hospital. Over the next twenty years the building was used for a variety of educational facilities until it was converted into a nursing home in 1979. Chickens and cows were kept in the grounds and fruit trees planted alongside veggie gardens to meet the needs of the hospital, and to generate income. However the coup d'état of September 12, 1980, saw an end to that.

In the following two decades a struggle began over whether the grounds and existing buildings should continue to be utilised for education, or further developed with new structures for tourism and other money-making projects. By 1998 the lines had been clearly drawn. On the one side were advocates of development and change and on the other was the Validebağ Yurttaş İnisiyatifini. The Validebağ Citizens' Initiative is a volunteer group made up of residents living in the nearby suburbs of Acıbadem, Koşuyolu, Altunizade and Barbaros.

In the ensuing years numerous legal battles were fought. Plans were drawn up to cut a road through part of the park lands and another to section off an area for the construction of private villas. Each time concerned citizens waded in, pooled resources and resisted what they saw as attacks on one of Istanbul's few green spaces. In one instance, well before there was a computer in nearly every home, they collected 6000 signatures in a single week. The result of their hard work is that the Validebağ Korusu remains open to all.

Evening classes are still held in Adile Sultan's former divan, now an *Öğretmenevi*, a teacher's house. It's where the famous *Hababam Sınıfı* (The Outrageous Class) series of movies was filmed. They starred the much-loved Kemal Sunal in the role of Şaban. In the films his classmates called him Inek Şaban, meaning cow Şaban, in reference to his bovine like eyes and placid nature. Inek Şaban was constantly bullied and humiliated by his friends, but this never kept him from thinking the unthinkable, like digging a tunnel to escape from the school grounds, which ultimately led to the vice-principal's office or smoking in the school attic. Hababam Sınıfı was enormously popular and the school room remains set up as it was during takes, with portraits of the cast propped up around the room. Naturally most people opt for a photo of themselves sharing the bench seat double desk with Şaban.

Outside there's a relaxing tea garden with tables and chairs scattered among a stand of mature trees where retired teachers and Turkish families come to sit and gossip. Follow the road off the carpark and you'll discover ten hectares of forest, full of easy-to-follow trails. Even though you do come across other people, even on busy weekends it feels just like you've walked off the streets of Istanbul and straight into the countryside. You'll pass oak, cypress, Japanese plum, coastal pines, quince, gum mastic and cedar trees, including Atlas and Himalayan, just to name some of the 40 different species in the reserve. They range in age from 15 to 400 years old, with 25 plant species in total. 119 species of birds call Validebağ home including migrating storks who have their very own section in the grounds, reserved just for them since 1986.

Address: the entry nearest to the Adile Sultan Pavilion is just down from the intersection of Tophanelioğlu Caddesi and Kalfa Çeşmesi Sokak, Altunizade.

Catch the dolmuş from Kadıköy that goes through Koşuyolu, Validebağ and Kapitol AVM. It leaves from the Kadıköy dolmuş transport hub on the waterfront. Tell the driver you want to get off at the Validebağ girişi (entry gate). Just those two words will be enough. To catch a dolmuş back to Kadıköy just cross over the road and wait till one comes along. Alternatively, if you want to visit the Marmara Üniversitesi İlahiyat Fakültesi Camii ve Kültür Merkezi (see page 108 for details about this mosque and culture centre) get on a dolmuş coming from the Kadıköy dolmuş transport hub (the same direction you originally came from) and tell the driver you want to get out at Capitol AVM. It's a big shopping centre one block up from the mosque.

EUROPEAN SIDE OF ISTANBUL

BEŞİKTAŞ

Şeyh Zafir Türbe

It's common to assume mosques are only places of worship and that all the people associated with them are Muslims. However during the reign of the Ottomans, Istanbul was a magnet for talent and believers of different faiths from all over the world. This fusion is often best seen in the architecture they left behind, like the Şeyh Zafir türbe.

Şeyh Zafir, or Sheikh Zafir was born near Tripoli in Libya in 1828 and died in Istanbul in 1903. He was a member of the Şâzelîlik, the Shadhili Tariqa Sufi order founded in the 13th century. It's widely practised around the world even today. Şeyh Zafir came to Istanbul in 1870, and there's various stories about how he got here, involving his brother Hamza and Pertevniyal Valide Sultan, the mother of Sultan Abdülhamid II (born 21 September 1842 and died 10 February 1918). No one's sure which version is actually true, but it's evident the sultan held Zafir in high esteem.

So much so he ordered the Ertuğrul Tekke complex be built in 1887-1888. It consists of a mosque of the same name, a tekke, a lodge where derviş could stay and a guest house. The mosque was named for Ertuğrul Gazi, father of Osman I, otherwise known as the founder of the Ottoman Empire. Abdülhamid II was determined to spread the word of unity through Pan Islamism as a way to deal with the multiple ethnicities living in Ottoman lands, and Şeyh Zafir played a significant role in North Africa.

Rather than being a religious base, Ertuğrul Tekke functioned as a political centre where visitors from Tripoli could stay. All their expenses were taken care of and their loyalty to the Empire encouraged through monetary grants and other means. The sultan came from his quarters in Yildiz Saray up the hill to perform his Friday prayers in the Selamlık, the men's section, making his support of Şeyh Zafir crystal clear.

The sultan looked after the whole Zafir family, including his wife and numerous children. When the sheikh died in 1903 Abdülhamid decided to commemorate him by having a special tomb designed. It was completed between 1905 and 1906 and is the work of Italian architect Raimondo D'Aronco, the man responsible for bringing Art Nouveau architecture to the city. He was born in Gemona del Friuli in 1857, by coincidence part of the region in Northern Italy my husband's family comes from. After primary school D'Aronco went to a local Arts and Crafts School for two years before being apprenticed to a master builder. From there he went to Venice to study Ornamental Design and Architecture at the Academy of Fine Arts. On graduation he started working and entered architectural competitions where his original and imaginative designs met with considerable success.

In 1893 Sultan Abdülhamid II requested the Italian government provide an architect to design an exhibition to mark his 20 years of rule. A devastating earthquake in 1894 put an end to the project but D'Aronco stayed on and oversaw inspections and repairs to damaged buildings. As the first ever foreign born palace architect Raimondo D'Aronco was also charged with remodelling part of the sultan's private residence.

He worked alongside Sarkis Balyan, a member of the famous Armenian family responsible for creating Dolmabahçe Palace. While the Balyans specialised in monumental grandeur, D'Aronco used Rococo exuberance combined with experimental Art Nouveau. This early work allowed him to explore ways to articulate Art Nouveau motifs together with Ottoman sensibilities and come up with unique and beautiful designs.

Consequently the Sheikh Zafir Tomb marks a huge shift in the aesthetics of Istanbul architecture. It's only small and sort of squished in between the larger mosque, rose gardens and an iron fence, but I took my time and examined it from all sides. The way D'Aronco combined Jugenstil, the German and Austrian versions of Art Nouveau rectilinear form, with the late Ottoman focus on small fanciful landmarks, is breathtaking. The tomb is both of its time and stylistically futuristic. I have plenty of words I can use to describe it but none of them beat seeing it in person.

Raimondo D'Aronco was prolific with his ideas but sadly many of his projects were never realised and exist only on paper. The tomb is one of the few buildings he was able to see fully completed. After Sultan Abdülhamid II was deposed in 1909 D'Aronco

Facade of the Şeyh Zafir tomb

returned to Italy and died in 1932. He avoided the limelight, never granted a press interview or boasted of his achievements and was by all accounts a humble man. Luckily for us he left behind a small but perfect architectural legacy. A fitting testimony to this extremely talented individual as well as its inhabitant.

Address: Mehmet Ali Bey Sokağı No 8, Beşiktaş

The street where the tomb sits is off Barbaros Bulvari in Beşiktaş. The quickest way to get there from Eminönü is by ferry. The complex is a bit over half a kilometre from the main square near the water, up a rather steep hill. It's not worth trying to get a taxi for this short distance but take it easy if you plan to visit in summer.

If you miss the ferry catch the tram from Eminönü to Kabataş. It's the last stop. From there you can get a 27E, 41E, 58A, 58N, 62 or 63 to the Barbaros Bulvarı bus stop. From the point you alight walk back down the hill and you'll see the mosque and tomb off to your left.

Yahya Efendi Türbesi

The tomb of Yahya Efendi lies in the Şeyh Yahya Efendi Külliyesi, the Sheik Yahya Efendi Social Complex, on a ridge overlooking the Bosphorus a short distance from Beşiktaş. Yahya Efendi was a famous scholar of the 16th century born in Trabzon in 1495. His year of birth coincided with that of Kanuni Sultan Süleyman, whose mother also breastfed Yahya Efendi, making them milk brothers. When prince Süleyman became the 10th Ottoman Sultan, otherwise known as Süleyman the Magnificent, Yahya Efendi became his advisor. Later in life Yahya Efendi bought the plot where the complex is located, and established a lodge to provide training and aid to the needy of Istanbul.

He was enormously popular during his lifetime and this carried over after his death on May 4, 1571.

Thousands of people attended Yahya Efendi's funeral and many of his followers and admirers wanted to be laid to rest alongside him. His tomb is adjacent to a mosque that was originally the lodge where Yahya Efendi lived and administered to the poor. When he died his grave was laid out beside it and then Ottoman Sultan Selim II had famous architect Mimar Sinan build a domed shrine around it. The entry to the shrine is along a walkway laid with stones, lined with gravestones inscribed with calligraphy and a fountain built by Sultan Abdülhamid II.

Yahya Efendi's tomb sits in an iron cage, surrounded by the sarcophagi of his wife and children. One side of the cage opens onto a small mosque officially called the Yavuz Sultan Selim Camii, also known as Selim II Camii. Most visitors pay scant attention to the mosque as their focus is on the tomb. Little boys dressed in princely robes preparing to undergo circumcision visit with their parents, pregnant women pray for a safe delivery, while those still hoping to be married or just in need of spiritual guidance stand in front of Yahya Efendi and ask for help in Allah's name. When their prayers are answered they return again to give thanks and leave gifts for the poor.

The complex has been rebuilt several times over the centuries after being decimated by fires and earthquakes. Sometime during its history the mosque has obviously been restored and provides enviable views over the water from a series of large windows along the front wall. The room has a low roof featuring elegant details in the many hanging chandeliers and painted wooden balconies and decorative ceiling.

In the late 19th century Sultan Abdülhamid II had a new shrine built to contain the princes and female family members of the Ottoman court. The fountain and library were restored during the same period and after the founding of the Turkish Republic in 1923, handwritten books dating back hundreds of years were sent from here to Süleymaniye library for safekeeping.

In addition to Yahya Efendi's immediate family and members of the Ottoman elite, state governors, judges, university lecturers and other educated and wealthy city residents are buried in the cemetery surrounding the main building. The cemetery takes up an area greater than that of the mosque and tomb. It's full of plane, cypress, willow and fir trees and more than 2500 Ottoman graves. If like me you have a penchant for graveyards, I suggest you walk to the top of the path and slowly work your way back down. There are dozens of female gravestones decorated with flowers and other traditional symbols, male gravestones topped with Ottoman *fez* and other markers from different sects such as the Mawlavi, Nakşibendi and Bektaşi. When you're finished there, walk around to the side of the mosque and follow the path leading to another level down, in front of the building. Your reward is marvellous views of the Bosphorus and the somewhat surreal scene of broken gravestones neatly laid out in rows.

Address: Intersection of Yahya Efendi Sokak and Çırağan Caddesi, Beşiktaş

Before you make your plans, be aware the road leading to the Yahya Efendi Türbesi is unbelievably steep. Walking up it is not pleasant when the temperature hits the high 30s. Depending on your level of fitness and preferences, you can walk there from Beşiktaş in about 15 minutes. Yahya Efendi Sokak (street) is a block along past the entry to Yıldız Park. Or pick up bus numbers 22, 25E, 40T from the Bahçeşehir Universite bus stop in Beşiktaş, travel two stops and get off at the Yahya Efendi bus stop. Once you're on the street look across the road to your left and you'll see a narrow street going straight up. Alternatively you can take a taxi.

Opening times: 06.45-21.45, 7 days a week

Yıldız Hamidiye Camii

From the outside Yıldız Hamidiye Camii looks just like an over-the-top wedding cake or traditional Christmas slice adorned with royal icing, the gleaming stylised sheets of frosting made from egg whites and sugar. It's a great piece of eye candy and the interior is even more impressive. Strangely, it doesn't appear on Instagram accounts or on lists of must visit mosques in Istanbul. The location might have something to do with it. The mosque sits almost at the top of Barbaros Caddesi, a steep stretch of road leading up from the waterfront at Beşiktaş all the way to Levent. It's a challenge for even the fittest and at the turn off there's another small hill to climb. By the time you walk past the security booths and armed guards protecting entry to parts of the Yıldız Palace complex adjacent, you're likely to need a sit down, especially on a typically hot Istanbul summer day.

Here's some information to take in while you have a seat and catch your breath. The mosque was built for Sultan Abdülhamid II and completed in 1886. He ruled from August 31, 1876 to April 27, 1909, when the Empire was under siege. Territorial holdings were shrinking fast as non-Turkic subjects rose up in protest and the Ottoman's reputation as world players was being usurped by the economic and technological growth of western nations. If they were to regain their position a new strategy was needed, still Islamic but open to modernity and difference. Naturally, Ottoman rulers would be at the helm.

Even before Abdülhamid II took over, architecture had been used as a way to express this. Buildings by the Armenian Balyan family, official architects to the court, such as Dolmabahçe Palace and Merasim Köşkü in Ihlamur Kasrı, combined western styles with classical Ottoman and Islamic traditions in a drive to show a new face to the public and to visitors from far off lands. This trend reached a peak during the Hamidian period, as Abdülhamid II's rule was known, as seen in the design of Yıldız Hamidiye Camii, the Hamidian Star Mosque. Unlike the European architectural influences clearly visible in the aforementioned structures, this mosque incorporated western Orientalist artistic styles, that is western ideas of what Islamic traditions should look like, along with Moorish influences and a touch of neo-Gothic thrown in.

Construction took two years. Chief architect Sarkis Balyan was the supervisor, assisted by Armenian architect Dikran Kalfa or Jüberian. The base of the mosque is made up of a series of block like rooms with a single dome on top of the main hall. It would be fairly plain if not for the neo-Gothic facade with detailing reminiscent of Mughal decals. The end result wouldn't look out of place in Brighton Pier.

The seemingly random mismatching of elements ends once you enter. Inside, Andalusian-influenced Moorish influences are evident everywhere. The walls are covered in vibrant blue and gold painted decals with handcrafted lattices made of cedar wood, fashioned by Sultan Abdülhamid II himself. He was inspired by the Alhambra in Granada, Spain and also referenced it in the design of the *minbar* he made. If permitted, that is you're female, head upstairs to the women's section located in what was formerly the sultan's lodge, the area reserved only for him. It offers the best view of all the details up close, including the dome. You can see how the deep blue colour of the walls subtly lightens until it becomes a paler blue dotted with stars made from gold foil, the circle lined with complimentary shades of pink and sunset hues.

Look out for inscriptions along the walls. They're written in the Kufic style of calligraphy (for more information see the Zühtü Paşa Camii entry on page 82) and are the work of Ebüzziya Mehmet Tevfik Bey. The medallion set into the centre of the dome

Yıldız Hamidiye Mosque interior

includes quotes from the Surah al-Mulk, that is verses from the Koran. A large chandelier sent as a gift by Kaiser Wilhelm II completes the décor. He's the same man the *Alman Çeşmesi*, the German Fountain in Sultanahmet was built for.

The mosque opened in 1886 and became the venue where Sultan Abdülhamid II attended Friday prayers. Previous sultans performed their Friday prayers in the larger and grander Hagia Sophia, Süleymaniye or Sultan Ahmed mosques. In Islam,

Friday midday prayers were the time when political statements and court decrees are announced. Back then, it was about the only time most people would ever get to see their leaders in the flesh, so huge crowds would gather. One Friday, July 21, 1905 to be exact, an attempt was made on Abdülhamid's life by the Dashnak organisation, the Armenian Revolutionary Federation. A bomb exploded but the sultan escaped untouched but 26 of his retinue died and another 58 members of the public were injured. Sultan Abdülhamid II was deposed four years later and died in 1918.

Yıldız Hamidiye was meant to be the mosque that would usher in a new dawn for the Ottomans, but instead was the last mosque ever built for a sultan in Istanbul. Although it only has one minaret with a single balcony, it's a fitting testimony to the grandeur of the past.

Address: Serencebey Yokusu No 63, Beşiktaş

As I mentioned before you can walk up the hill but you can also catch a bus. From the Beşiktaş Meydanı bus stop take a 27E, 43R, 58A, 58N or 62 two stops up the hill. Get out at Yıldız Teknik Üniversitesi stop and then walk back down the way you've come until you see a turn off and a park on your left. The street is Saray Caddesi and it leads around to the mosque. Once you see the Yıldız Saat Kulesi (a clock tower) built in 1890 to commemorate 25 years of reign by Sultan Abdülhamid, you've arrived.

BOSPHORUS

Baltalimanı Japon Bahçesi

Japanese gardens providing a quiet respite from the city

Today, Baltalimanı, which means 'axe port' in Turkish, is just another neighbourhood on the shores of the Bosphorus but in 1838 it was where an important trade agreement was signed between Great Britain and the Ottoman Sublime Porte. The Treaty of Balta Limanı gave both countries the right to trade in each other's territories with assorted beneficial terms and conditions included. It was signed first by Queen Victoria and then by Sultan Mahmut II. Less well known is that the area is home to a small traditional Japanese garden, commemorating 30 years of friendship between Istanbul and the city of Shimonoseki, Yamaguchi Province, in the Kamon Straits of Japan.

2003 was the year of Japan in Turkey and planning for the gardens began in 2001. To cement the importance of the connection, Japanese designers and workers came to Istanbul to create a garden using elements from important architectural sites of Shimonoseki itself. It's very authentic with many of the materials used brought over from Japan. The traditional large entrance gate with heavy tiled peak roof is based on the gates of the Chofu Garden, and inside there are tranquil ponds, a small traditional Japanese tea house, waterfalls, and wooden pergola. The grounds are full of native plants and flowers from Japan such as maples and a famous *sakura*, a cherry tree.

Initially the Baltalimanı Japanese Gardens were very popular and saw lots of visitors but over the years they became neglected. When Istanbul was awarded the role of European Capital of Culture in 2010, the Istanbul Municipality together with that of Shimonoseki restored them to their former tranquil beauty. Further work was done in November 2015, this time to commemorate a tragedy that had occurred 125 years previously. In 1890 the Ottoman Navy frigate Ertuğrul hit a reef and sank off the coast of the Wayayama Prefecture when returning from a goodwill voyage to Japan. 500 sailors and officers drowned, but the 69 who survived were returned to Turkey aboard two Japanese corvettes.

My favourite part of the grounds is the raked stone and gravel garden. They're called *karesansui*, meaning dry landscapes in Japan, and were developed in the late Kamakira period between 1185 and 1333. The aesthetics of the design are based on the principle of *yohaku-no-bi*, the beauty of blank space, something which is very rare in Istanbul. These gardens are often referred to as Zen gardens because they are frequently laid out in Zen monasteries in Japan as places of quiet contemplation.

Address: Sakıp Sabancı Caddesi No 76, Baltalimanı

The gardens are quite a way up the Bosphorus but you can now get a ferry from Üsküdar to Aşiyan and from there catch a bus 22, 22RE, 40T or 42T three stops to the Baltalimanı bus stop. You can also get those buses from their starting points at Kabataş and Taksim, but you'll spend more than an hour in traffic. The ferries are every hour after 9am (9.15, 10.15 etc) and run more frequently after 15.15pm. The trip takes 25 minutes and you get to enjoy the Bosphorus at the same time.

Opening times: 08.00-19.00 in summer, 08.00-17.00 in winter. 7 days a week. Free entry.

EMINÖNÜ AND SURROUNDING NEIGHBOURHOODS

Ahmet Hamdi Tanpınar Edebiyat Müze Kütüphanesi

In Gülhane Park, stretching down the hill from Sultanahmet almost to the point where the waters of the Bosphorus meet the Sea of Marmara, monumental plane trees, well-established walnut and oaks stand guard along wide pathways wending past colourful flower beds and an ornamental pond. The Park of the Rose House as it translates in English is particularly popular in summer, with families and tourists seeking respite from the heat while courting couples head for private nooks where they can sit close together and whisper sweet nothings to one another.

In their haste most people walk straight past Alay Köşk, the Procession Kiosk, built onto the outer wall of the park just beside the largest entryway. English architect William Smith built it in Baroque style in 1853 or 1854 for Sultan Abdülmecid I as part of the original grounds of Topkapı Palace. This was the only building in the whole complex with windows overlooking the street, in a room known as the Domed Hall. The sultan would sit on long brocade cushions lining the seats beneath the windows to watch the Janissary troops parade past as he saluted them.

The köşk was also a place for pleasure and relaxation but these days it's home to the Ahmet

Hamdi Tanpınar Literature Museum and Library. Ahmet Hamdi Tanpınar was a Turkish literary great, creating and writing many poems, literary critiques, novels and essays during his lifetime. Born on 23 June 1901, like many Turks he had a finger in several pies, serving as a member of the Turkish Parliament between 1944 and 1946. By the time he died on 24 January 1962 he was considered the greatest representative of modernism in Turkish literature. His best-known work for readers in English is *A Mind at Peace* (first published in Turkish under the title *Huzur*, in 1949).

Entry to the library is via a stone ramp and leads to rooms that are polygon in shape with highly polished floors that creak gloriously as you walk across them. All of them have hand painted ceilings, ruby glass chandeliers, and large wood framed windows yet each room is different in some way. Some contain collections of ephemera such as typewriters, pipes and letter openers used by famous Turkish writers and even personal items belonging to Ayşe Kulin and Zülfü Livaneli. A few contain fanciful *trompe l'oeil* panels illustrated with scenes harking back to rural France. Everywhere you look there are shelves packed with local histories, novels, magazines and slim volumes of poetry. Turn a corner and you come face to face with famous Turkish literary figures like the library's namesake, along with Nobel Laureate Orhan Pamuk and world famous poet Nazim Hikmet represented in larger than life size busts.

The library briefly housed a Fine Arts Association in the early 20th century. However from 1928 until the end of the 1930s it was where Tanpınar and his contemporaries came together as the Council Literature Association dedicated to Turkish language and literature. In 2011 the building was reopened as the Ahmet Hamdi Tanpınar Library containing more than 8000 books in Turkish and other languages from around 1000 authors. It includes city guides, award winning titles and even letters written by foreign ambassadors appointed to Istanbul. Readers are welcome to peruse the material in the library.

A main salon used for meetings, discussions and readings is housed on the lower floor but my favourite discovery was a little circular room full of vinyl records from the 1960s and 70s. They weren't music recordings though. Rather they were recitations of Turkish poetry in both Turkish and English, with names like "The Voice of Turkish Authors", and included works by Yunus Emre, among others.

Back upstairs the Domed Hall contains works by local writers housed in long low bookcases. Opposite this is a smaller, plainer room equipped with a just few tables and chairs. If you're lucky and there's a seat free, it's the perfect spot to sit and work on your own literary masterpiece. Or a place to drowse dreamily in the afternoon sun and well, do nothing at all.

Address: Alay Köşkü, Gülhane Parkı İçi No 1,
Eminönü/Sirkeci

Follow the tram track up from Eminönü or down
from Sultanahmet and enter via the gate just near the
Gülhane tramstop.

Opening times: 08.30-19.00, Mon–Sat. Closed
Sundays.

Ali Muhiddin Hacı Bekir

Address: Hamidiye Caddesi No 31-33, Eminönü
(near the Yeni Camii)

See page 32 for more information.

Beta Yeni Han

The streets of Eminönü are packed with tiny shops
selling an enormous variety of goods from party
fancies and bubble wrap through to hand worked
copper trays and tin water jugs. Everywhere you
look it's wall-to-wall people, especially inside the
Mısır Çarşısı (the Egyptian Bazaar) and the corner
opposite. That's where hundreds of people line up
every day to buy a packet (or five) of the famous
Kurukahveçi Mehmet Efendi Turkish coffee. It's
located at the start of a long narrow street called
Hasırcılar Sokak, Canemaker's Street, and you can
still find items made from cane at the very end.

I love spending time here but eventually, constantly
having to duck out of the way of *hamal*, Turkish

porters carrying huge loads on their backs (including washing machines) and multi-generation family groups out doing wedding shopping, gets to me. You know the kind, the ones who stop suddenly, form impassable human walls and basically get in everyone's way. One minute I'm having fun, next I'm exhausted and desperate to sit down somewhere quiet for a while.

After a morning running errands in the area I was about ready to drop. Although I still had things to get I was thinking of calling it a day and catching a ferry home for a nap. Then quite by chance, during a brief lull in the constant stream of people, I happened to look right and caught the eye of a young girl dressed in black pants and formal white shirt. She beckoned me over and offered me a brochure, advertising more types of tea than I knew existed. Behind her, along a short narrow passageway was a large courtyard I'd never noticed before.

Variously called Emin Han, Tahmis Han and Hasırcılar Han as well as Yeni Han, this centuries old commercial centre reopened its doors in 2019 as Beta Yeni Han. The original foundations were laid in the early 17th century but it took its final form as a two story building under the auspices of the Kazasker Abdulkadir Efendi foundation in 1671. The upper floor was lost in a fire and the rest of the structure was severely damaged in an earthquake in 1894. For decades the rooms and central space were used for storage but eventually became the resting place for unwanted objects, discarded junk and plain old rubbish. Consequently I'd passed it dozens of times before without ever noticing it.

Interior of Beta Yeni Han

The word *tahmis* means coffee roasting and this site is believed to be the first place coffee was processed, stored, roasted and ground in Istanbul. Restorations revealed the original coffee roasting stove and grinding area in what is now the basement of the building. Entrance to this is via the Beta Tea House. They sell umpteen types of tea but make very good coffee too, whether it's traditionally Turkish or my preference, a double espresso with hot milk on the side. The tea house was designed to fit with the original structure so the architects created a false floor of thick Perspex to reveal and protect the original stonework underfoot. The walls have been left unplastered, showcasing the hand-hewn stone and bricks dating back many years. A clear roof overhead means that even on the dullest of days the space is light filled and airy, giving it a lovely otherworldly feel.

Address: Hasırcılar Caddesi No 23, Tahtakale, Eminönü
Opening times: 07.30-20.00, Sat-Thur, 14.00-20.00, Fri

Kurukahveçi Mehmet Efendi

See page 57 for more information.

Address: Tahmis Sokak No 66, Eminönü

TCDD İstanbul Demiryolu Müzesi

The one room railway museum at Sirkeci Railway Station in Istanbul is a ferroequinologist's (a humorous name for someone who studies trains as a hobby) delight. In fact, even people like me who see trains simply as a useful form of transport will find lots to enjoy here. First there's the station itself. It was built in 1888 by German architect August Jasmund and opened in 1890. Jasmund was a graduate of the University of Berlin and came to Istanbul to study Oriental architecture. He crossed paths with Sultan Abdüilhamid II and was soon made the consultant architect of the Ottoman court.

Although the main structure has seen better days, the architectural features employed by Jasmund to reflect the station's position as the point where the West ended and the East began are still extant. The walls are made from marble and stone imported from the Arden in Marseille. The two materials were deliberately laid in a combination creating horizontal bands along the façade, in recognition of regional and national patterns found throughout Turkey. The overall look is Oriental-Gothic while the pointed arched windows inset with the original round stained glass windows are similar to the designs found in stone doors of the Selçuk period. The entire building sits on a base made from granite.

All this grandeur is fitting for what was and is again the last stop on the famous Orient Express. The idea for a long distance train was first touted in 1865 by Georges Nagelmackers, the son of a Belgian Banker. While over in America he'd seen George Pullman's innovative train sleeper cars and returned determined to establish the same in Europe. He set up his own company, the Compagnie Internationale des Wagons-Lits (*wagons-lits* is French for sleeper cars) and on October 4, 1883 the first ever Orient Express, a name given by the press, left Paris. It carried around 40 passengers headed for Giurgiu in Romania, via Munich and Vienna. From there passengers were ferried across the Danube to Rousse in Bulgaria where another train was waiting to take them to the coastal town of Varna. Then they boarded another ship bound for Istanbul. At the time there was no single unified rail system through Europe, and none at all in many of the countries the train traversed. The first truly non-stop Paris-Constantinople (as Istanbul was then known) train ran in 1889 and continued until 1977.

By then the once majestic train had fallen on hard times. Only hippies travelling overland to Asia and traders made the journey. They had to bring their own food because the dining room had long been closed. Although the Orient Express might have been down it wasn't out, and in the following decades the service was revitalised and renewed. Once again the train departs from Paris, bound for the Sirkeci Railway Station in Istanbul.

Driver's cabin from TCDD suburban train

The railway museum in Sirkeci Station opened in 2005 and displays original silver services used on the Orient Express and furniture, including a fixed table and swivel chair set from the dining car. Sadly they've replaced the groovy Thunderbirds Are Go original upholstery with something much plainer, but they still appeal. The glass cabinets are crammed with printed menus, commemorative medals presented to passengers on the final service in 1977, advertising posters and the like. The museum also contains historical memorabilia from the Türkiye Cumhuriyeti Devlet Demiryolları, that's the Turkish Republic Public Railways or TCDD for short. Items like train conductors' bags, ticket dispensing units, pocket watches with trains on them and memorabilia from the Turkish State Railways hospital have all been preserved. The walls are covered in train manufacturers' plates, railway maps, framed photographs and sets of commemorative stamps with a different type of engine on each one. There's even a complete driver's cabin set up in the middle of the room. Not from just any train. It's from a TCDD suburban train and symbolises the transition to the first ever electric trains in Turkey in 1955. Speaking of electric trains, there's even a Hornby electric train set, complete with railway carriages and moving parts.

Address: Sirkeci Gar (Railway Station), Eminönü

The location of the museum makes it easy to visit when you're on your way to or from somewhere else. It's just down the hill from the Ahmet Hamdi Tanpınar Literature Museum and Library in Gulhane Park and just up from the Eminönü waterfront where you can catch a ferry across to Kadıköy or Üsküdar.

Opening hours: 09.30-17.00, Tue-Sun. Closed Mondays. Free entry.

Türkıye Iş Bank Müzesi

Visiting the Türkıye Iş Bank Müzesi in Eminönü took me back to my primary school years in Australia. I can still remember a man from the bank standing in our classroom telling us all about the merits of saving. Or some such thing. Truth be told, as an eight year old I was more interested in the

Ottoman money box

shiny tin models of the national bank sitting in tempting rows, ready to be handed out when the man ever stopped talking. The Ottoman versions of moneyboxes in the Turkish Iş Bank Museum look much sturdier than my first one. Granted, it could only be cut open at the bank but I suspect the Turkish versions would require a blow torch followed by vigorous use of a hacksaw.

The museum has three levels of fascinating banking paraphernalia on display, and even though there are no English translations of the descriptions, it's well worth a visit. There are postcards from the 1930s showing children how to save, as well as cartoon ads from the 1940s. My favourite is the one showing a money box with a cigarette in its hand.

Early on Iş Bank understood the importance of branding. They produced student notebooks, presumably to give away, with the bank logo, picture and cartoons on the covers. Even today, at a table set up to show how their advertising section worked, you can stamp a picture on a piece of paper with an Iş Bank header to take home as a souvenir. There are dozens of posters from the 20th century about the benefits of saving, new branch openings and buying houses on credit. There's a selection of television ads featuring Turkish fashion designers such as Vitali Hakko, the man behind the Vakko label and actors like Cem Yilmaz. He portrays famous director, actor and producer Servet Bey who made early advertisements for the bank. They even screen the first Bankamatik ads from 1982.

One section is dedicated to original bank fixtures such as teller booths and other furnishings. However my favourite area was downstairs in the vault. To reach it you have to follow a long corridor with hundreds of numbers projected on the floor. They move like figures scrolling down an old-fashioned computer screen. There are sounds effects too, of coins clinking and the flicking noise of paper money being counted by machines at high speed. Theses audio visual effects are a bit disconcerting and can throw you off balance, especially when someone suddenly appears around the corner. When this happened to me, the woman I nearly ran into and I simultaneously jumped in fright because we weren't expecting to see anyone else. Then we laughed with relief.

There's a room full of bank deposit boxes at the end of this corridor. Some slots have been left open and only show the face of the locked boxes while others are screened with Perspex, to protect and reveal the personal treasures kept inside – cut glass perfume bottles, Meerschaum pipes and battered but much loved toys. Further on there are massive safes with doors a foot or more thick.

I'm not big on numismatics, the study or collection of monetary paraphernalia, but as a writer and sociologist I am interested in people and culture. I not only relived a bit of my childhood at the Iş Bank Museum I also learned quite a lot about Turkish society, especially in the early to mid-twentieth century.

Address: Bankacılar Sokak No 2, Eminönü

The museum is located behind the Yeni Camii, not far from Mısır Çarşi, the Egyptian or Spice Bazaar. It's in a grand salmon pink and cream building but it is still possible to miss the entrance if you get caught up in a crush of people. I don't know how many times I passed it without realising what's inside.

Opening times: 10.00-18.00 Tue–Sun. Closed Mondays. Free entry.

FATIH

II Bayezid Türk Hamam Kültürü Müzesi

When you follow the tramway line in the direction of Aksaray, away from Sultanahmet, the city's past is written in solid blocks of creamy gold coloured sandstone. Quiet, ordinary entries to mosques, sombre university auditoriums and nondescript walls sheltering elegant cemeteries beckon. At the point where the street heads downhill however, you have to know to stop and look up if you don't want to miss the II Bayezid Türk Hamam Kültürü Müzesi, the Bayezid II Turkish Bath Culture Museum. This vast stone structure presents only a blank wall to passing pedestrians, but climb the stairs and it's a different story.

The Bayezid II Turkish Hamam was built between 1501 and 1506 as part of the larger Bayezid Külliye, a type of Muslim social complex. It is the largest Turkish bath in Istanbul. Unlike many which only allow entry to men and women on different days because they only contain one bathing facility, the Bayezid II bath had double sections for men and women, meaning either sex could bathe on the day of their choice.

Entry to the museum is through a high pointed arched gate leading to the vast men's *camekan*, also called a *söyunmalık*. The dome here is 15 metres in diameter and this is where bathers would change in dressing rooms one level up, anchored to the walls. The women's section opens onto a side street and is identical in design, although the overall space and windows are smaller.

The route through the displays follows the path bathers take in a traditional hamam. Undressed and wrapped only in a *peştemal,* a striped wrap woven from soft cotton, you would pass through the square *soğukluk*, the cold room, walk around a corner into the *ılıklık eyvanı*, a domed room heated to a lukewarm temperature, before finally reaching the *sıcaklık eyvanı,* a well heated large central space with smaller rooms and alcoves off it. The idea is to acclimatise your body to both the change in temperature and atmosphere. By the time you reach this last space, your breathing has slowed and your mind too, providing psychological as well as physical benefits. When I lived in Kayseri, in central Anatolia, I spent many hours lying on the *göbek taşı*, the raised platform made of marble in the centre of this space, being pleasantly pummelled and scrubbed while gazing into the bowl of the dome overhead. That hamam dated to the Selçuk period, making it older than the Bayezid II bath, and it was far more basic in terms of design and facilities.

In the past, everything owned by bathers was brought to the hamam wrapped in specially embroidered cloths. They held an assortment of items such as towels, soaps with the sultan's *tuğra*, his personal insignia stamped on them, combs and even Turkish coffee sets. Along with *peştemal*, bathers used separate towels to wrap around hair and shoulders or to place on the marble benches.

The higher the owner's position in the sultan's court the more expensive the material and decoration.

Special hamam shoes called takunya

Thick gold braid, fine silver wire, tiny sparkly beads individually sewn into place and carefully oversewn silk threads were worked into them, creating abstract patterns, idyllic rural scenes or floral fancies.

Hamam floors are always wet, whether from steam or from bathers pouring water over themselves using custom made *hamam tası*, silver or tin lined copper bowls decorated with elaborately worked motifs. Those belonging to the very wealthy even had precious jewels inserted into the centre. To avoid getting their feet wet, women wore specially designed hamam shoes called *takunya*. Made of wood and decorated with elaborate filigree silver or inlaid with mother-of-pearl, they also signalled the wearer's status. Some of the ones on display here have teeth, the support stands holding the base board where the foot goes, 30 centimetres high.

Each room contains different toilet articles and my love of textiles and ornament was richly rewarded. I was particularly taken by the *topuk taşı* used for exfoliating the skin. For my hamam visits I had my own *kese,* a coarse mitt used to scrub dead skin from the body that I'd give to the kese woman to use on me. It did the job but was nowhere near as attractive as these pumice stones with casings made from silver or baked red clay, with beautifully modelled animals such as crocodiles or hippopotamus forming their grips.

Hamam accoutrements and also the culture and history of bathing are extremely well curated in the Bayezid II Museum. Some pieces on display date back several hundred years. Original wall patterns discovered during restoration were cleaned up and put on display and plaster copies made to achieve the full effect. Bits of marble are propped up in the *halvet*, the hottest rooms in the hamam where you go to sweat before exfoliating and then washing yourself clean. *Seki*, the bathing platforms along the walls of the eyvan still have *kurna*, heavy marble basins for water, in place. History abounds.

There's even an area dedicated to foreigners who visited Istanbul during the reign of the Ottomans.

Copies of etchings and prints hang on the walls alongside quotes from writers such as the famous correspondent Lady Mary Wortley Montagu and Edmondo di Amicis. He wrote about nymph like figures flitting through the dimly lit steam rooms of the marble interior in the hamam. That was in the 1870s though I doubt he actually saw them for himself. I suspect in truth the reality was much less exotic, and a lot closer to my experiences of multi-generational family groups in all assorted shapes and sizes. There was definitely no flitting in Kayseri but lots of laughter, especially if my visit coincided with a bridal bath. These were hamam outings where the bride and groom's families, including all their close female relatives, met in the bathhouse to sweat, eat and enjoy themselves. Once always held on a Tuesday, two days before the wedding, with the onset of modernity the tradition is dying out.

Address: Corner of Ordu Caddesi (tramway street) and Kimyager Derviş Paşa Sokak, Laleli

I love to walk so when the sun is shining, even on a cold winter day, I walk here from Sultanahmet. Just follow the Kabataş-Bağcılar tram tracks. If you're not so keen or are pressed for time, the closest tram stop to the museum is Laleli-Üniversite.

Opening times: 09.00-16.30, Mon–Fri. Closed weekends. Free entry.

Kadınlar Pazarı

Itfaiye Caddesi (Fire Department Street) in the Fatih district of Istanbul reminds me of the Turkey I encountered when I travelled through the country's heartland on my own in 1990. It still retains the open friendliness that delighted my husband when he first came to Turkey with me in 1996 and reminds me of the fun we had exploring the east of the country in the early 2000s. Back then foreign tourists rarely ventured beyond Anakara and Cappadocia. Even though our Turkish was pretty basic at the time, we met and talked to lots of different people from tiny villages and bigger towns wherever we went. We laughed and learned a lot and visited fabulous *pazar,* weekly local outdoor markets. Naturally we ate delicious food all the time, sometimes too much in one go, but it was impossible to say no.

Kadınlar Pazarı, as the street is more commonly known, is built next to the arches of the ancient *Bozdoğan Kemeri*, the Valens Aqueduct dating to the 4th century AD. Until 1908 the area was largely home to workers in *Zeyrek Çırçır*, a cotton mill. A fire in 1908 razed over 2500 houses in the district, making more than 20,000 people homeless. The current square and layout of the streets date to that time. From the 1960s through to the 1990s Kadınlar Pazarı was home to a fresh vegetable and fruit market. Just how the neighbourhood came to be called the Women's Market is unclear, but there are three different stories. The most popular version although unsavoury is that female slaves were sold here during the Ottoman Empire. Turkish historians confirm women were traded as commodities but believe they were sold in a location the other side of the hill, in or near the Haseki Complex. The complex housed the first women's hospital known in the world, something I find quite ironic given its

An unexpected visitor in Kadınlar Pazarı

history. In the 17th century the slave market moved to a *han* called Esirciler, Tavukpazarı. On today's maps that would make it close to Nuruosmaniye Mosque near the Grand Bazaar.

A second suggestion is that at one point in time only women shopped here so it was a safe place for them to come. I can't vouch for that but a third and lesser known story could also be true. Apparently wealthier city residents normally bought their fruit and vegetables in Eminönü and any produce not sold was gathered up by poor women who sold it from a spot next to the Hacı Kadın Hamamı (a Turkish bath for women) just west of the modern day Yenikapı Marmaray Station. Eventually they moved to Kadınlar Pazarı but I couldn't find any details as to why they moved location and when. Famous Moroccan scholar and explorer Ibn Battuta claims to have seen numerous shops run by women when he was in Istanbul, but he didn't specify which parts of the city he was talking about.

Towards the end of the 20th century people from eastern Turkey, particularly Siirt as well as Adıyaman and Mardin, started moving to Istanbul. Mostly low-income earners working in factories and the textile industry gravitated to the area and it soon became a meeting point for migrants. Kadınlar Pazarı became the focal point for people wanting to meet up with others from the same village or town, ask about job opportunities and catch up on news from home.

Like migrants everywhere, they brought their traditions with them. The commercial section of Kadınlar Pazarı is only short, but it's packed with shops selling honey from huge open pans or on the comb and dried herbs by the kilo. There are tables groaning with stacks of *otlu peynir,* white cheese with herbs and towers of hand pressed soaps, each colour designating a different use. Woven baskets overflow with dates from far flung places, half-a-dozen types of raisins and an array of spices in every colour of the rainbow and more. There are sweets of all sorts, slabs of *helva*, sheets of *peştil,* a chewy snack most often made from apricots cooked into a pulpy mass before being spread out thinly to dry and layers and layers of *çevizli sucuk*. The most traditional of these contain walnuts that have been immersed in a molasses mixture and left to set. The end results look like a sausage but they are fairly sweet. Other versions, using different ingredients, are even more so.

However the star of the show when it comes to Kadınlar Pazarı is meat. The further down the street you go the more butcher shops you'll see alongside dozens of *ocakbaşı lokantası*, grill restaurants. People from south east Turkey eat a lot of meat, and few parts of an animal are off limits. If offal isn't your thing or you're the tiniest bit squeamish, be warned. I have a pretty strong stomach but the sight of a bull's head, it's tongue protruding, was almost too much for me. Nonetheless it didn't stop me from eating *büryan kebab*, Kadınlar Pazarı's most famous dish. *Büryan kebab* is lamb slow-cooked in a *tandir* oven until the flesh is so tender it slides off the bone. *Perde pilau*, rice cooked in butter, pine nuts and almonds, wrapped in buttery dough and cooked in the oven is the perfect accompaniment. As of course is *içli köfte*, elliptical casings made from bulgur wheat and stuffed with minced veal and nuts. *Bumbar*, sometimes called *mumbar*, also goes well. It's a type of sausage from Siirt made from cow intestine stuffed with rice, thin slices of meat and well-seasoned, then sewn up and boiled until cooked through. It might sound off-putting but it's thoroughly washed and cleaned before use, just like the intestine covering the sausages you buy at your local butcher or supermarket back home. As I said before, meat is the main event in Kadınlar Pazarı but when it comes to dining, most of the restaurants like everywhere in Turkey, offer a good array of legume soups and vegetable side dishes.

A visit to Kadınlar Pazarı lets you experience a different face of Istanbul. Depending on the time of day, women often outnumber men in their quest for the perfect food item. They travel in pairs or groups, trailing grandmothers, aunties and small children. Whatever the hour, men dressed in smart waistcoats and traditional baggy pants called *şalvar* sit on low stools drinking tea through a sugar cube held between their teeth. The air is full of the smell of grilling meat and the sound of animated conversations in Turkish and Kurdish, with some Arabic mixed in.

Address: Itfaiye Caddesi, Fatih

Catch a 32, 336E, 36E, 38E or 90 from the Eminönü bus terminal and alight at Fatih İtfaiye-Şehit Taner Çebi stop. When you get off look towards the park where a road cuts it in two. Follow this under and through the aqueduct and you've arrived in Kadınlar Pazarı.

Kıztaşı

I was terrible at history in high school. All I came remember is having to memorise a series of dates and although I can still recite my childhood phone number, historical events mean nothing to me until I see them in the flesh, so to speak. That's not hard to do in Istanbul because unless you look where you're going, more than likely you'll stumble over or come across something dating back hundreds of years.

Like the Marcian Column. Called Kıztaşı in Turkish, this Roman honorific column dedicated to the Emperor Marcian who lived from 450 to 457 AD, now it sits in the middle of a roundabout in the Fatih district. It's one of only four surviving Byzantine columns in the city, and was unknown to Western historian and visitors until 1675. That's when French doctor and archaeologist Jacob Spon and English clergyman and travel writer George Wheeler 'rediscovered' it. I suspect that as far as the residents of the city were concerned the column was never really lost as such, given they found it in somebody's private garden. When a fire broke out in 1908 and presumably burnt down the dwelling where the column was residing, a plan was formed to provide it with a more suitable setting.

Unlike some of the other columns in the city you can walk right up to the Marcian and admire the carved red-grey Egyptian granite, and base encased in white marble. Truth be told the granite's more on the grey side these days. Three sides of the marble are carved with monograms within medallions, and the column is Corinthian in style. This just means the capital at the top is ornately decorated with carvings of foliage. An inscription in Latin reads "Principis hanc satuam Maciani, Cerne Tovuque Praefectus Vovit, Quod Tatianus Opus", informing us the Prefect Tatianus had the column erected in honour of Emperor Marcian. Originally there was a statue of Marcian on the top. It's long gone, whereabouts unknown, although the eagles around the base of his plinth are still in place.

Marcian's column is a convenient landmark and a great place for local lads to hang out with their mates. Maybe they're waiting for a pretty girl to walk past. After all, Kıztaşı means Girl's Stone in English. According to one theory the column was so named due to the figure of Venus on the base. This meant it was confused with another more famous column nearby, the Column of Venus. Venus was the Roman Goddess of love, sex, beauty and fertility and her column was believed to be imbued with the power to determine whether a girl was a virgin or not. The importance of being a virgin was a sacred matter, and those considered true virgins, such as the Vestals, had considerable divine and actual powers. I'm just not sure how a column could identify false virgins from real ones. Whatever the truth of the matter, somehow I don't think the boys I saw had history on their minds.

Address: Intersection of Kıztaşi Caddesi, Kizanlik Caddesi and Yeşil Tekke Kuyulu Sokak, İskenderpaşa, Fatih

The column is in a street leading off Macar Kardeşler Caddesi, which passes Kadınlar Pazarı, an easy walk from Veznecilar Metro stop. Alternatively catch a 31E, 336E, 37E or 38E from the Eminönü bus terminal and alight at Fatih İtfaiye-Şehit Taner

Çebi stop. Continue walking in the same direction as the bus and then turn left at Kıztaşi Caddesi.

Mimar Sinan Türbesi

Located on a street named after the great man himself, the tomb of Mimar Sinan, head architect to Sultan Süleyman aka Süleyman the Magnificent, comes as something of a surprise. Given it's just the other side of the boundary wall of his masterpiece Süleymaniye Camii, you'd expect something as majestic as the mosque itself, properly befitting an architect of Sinan's reputation. Instead, his tomb is in a small wedge-shaped plot of land, at the junction of two streets in front of the Eski Ağlar Kapısı. The exterior is bounded by marble perimeter walls and the inside busy with tombs and assorted greenery. Sinan's tomb is clearly visible through a metal grill set into the wall, and the entry is from the street heading down hill. The honeycomb building on the corner is a *sebil,* a public fountain for the free distribution of water. Next to it, the words "Mimar Sinan Türbesi 1490 to 1588" are carved on a simple plaque. If you continue down the slope you'll see signs on the left hand side for a cafe offering extensive views over the Golden Horn.

No one is sure whether Sinan or Joseph as he was originally named, was born to Greek or Armenian parents but most people agree they were Christians. Jospeh followed into his father's trade and trained as a stone mason and carpenter until he entered the Janissary corps. After converting and taking a Muslim name, Sinan became a construction officer in the Ottoman army, which is where his architectural talents came to light. His initial designs were for military bridges and fortifications, then he completed his first civilian project in 1539. Over the next 40 years he went on to design and oversee the construction of 79 mosques, 55 schools, more than 30 palaces and public baths, as well as numerous other structures such as bridges, aqueducts and hospitals throughout the Ottoman Empire.

The majority of Mimar Sinan's work took place in the Ottoman capital of Turkey, and it is largely his hand and those he inspired that created the enduring image of Istanbul as a city full of engineering marvels, architectural wealth and overwhelming grandeur. In contrast his tomb is very modest and unassuming. Sinan designed and constructed it himself, one year before his death. Seen from above, the layout looks exactly like a compass, such as those architect's use to draw circles. Perhaps this very simplicity combined with that touch of whimsy are a lasting indication of Sinan's real character.

Address: Mimar Sinan Caddesi No 52, Süleymaniye

Mimar Sinan's tomb is adjacent to the north corner of Süleymaniye Mosque. The best way to approach it depends where you're coming from, and your energy levels. It's only a 10-minute walk from Rüstem Paşa Camii down near the waterfront at Eminönü. I mention this mosque because I try to pop in whenever I'm passing as I can't the enough of the tile work. You'll need to look this route up on Google Map and screenshot it before you go. Be aware it's mainly uphill in a major shopping area so the streets can get extremely crowded. Otherwise I suggest you visit the tomb after you've sated your senses at Süleymaniye Mosque.

Opening times: Officially the tomb is meant to be open from 08.00-18.00, 7 days a week, unless closed for cleaning, but in reality, you can only see Mimar Sinan's tomb from the outside. Being located at a small but busy intersection there are always cars parked around it. It's difficult to get a good photo but don't let this put you off paying your respects to the individual behind many of Turkey's most glorious and innovative mosques.

Şehzade Camii and Külliyesi

I have a serious passion for mosques no matter the size, age or importance, but when it comes to Şehzade Camii it's the türbe that take my breath away. The tombs are enclosed behind a small nondescript wall accessed through a door that often sticks. The façade gives no inkling of the exquisite monuments showcasing the skills and flair of the architect and the artisans who created the tiles and interiors, particularly the one where the young man for whom the complex is named lies at eternal rest.

The şehzade in question, the son of a Sultan, was Prince Mehmet. He died from small pox in 1543, aged only 22. His father Süleyman the Magnificent saw in him a future leader and was devastated by his death. Süleyman is said to have mourned beside his son's body for three days. When he finally arose he'd decided to build a great mosque and pious foundation in Mehmet's memory. He commissioned architect Mimar Sinan to design it, and work started immediately. The complex opened in 1548 and was comprised of the mosque, tomb, a *medrese*, a *tabhane*, a hospice and an *imaret*, a soup kitchen.

Prince Mehmet's octagonal türbe, also designed by Mimar Sinan, is the largest of all the tombs in the walled garden and the most exquisite. Slender columns frame a small portico leading to a door with an inscription over the entrance portal. Written in Persian, it suggests the interior is akin to Paradise. Rare Iznik tiles in floral patterns of apple green and lemon yellow made using *cuerda seca,* a technique where line decorations are painted onto tile using a mixture of wax and colour, line the walls. Tiles of

The interior of Şehzade Mosque

this type were only produced in Turkey for around thirty years. Panes of Turkish stained glass sit above them, below a dome embellished by a central medallion adorned with painted red brick coloured foliage cascading over the surface, shadowed by smaller repetitions of the same design.

Süleyman's daughter Humaşah Sultan, his son Cihangir and other famous names from Ottoman history are buried here too such as the Grand Vezir Rüstem Paşa, the name behind my favourite mosque in Istanbul. Each is worth a close inspection as collectively they display some of the finest examples of tiles from the two best periods of tile production in Turkey.

The mosque itself is considered amongst Sinan's greatest achievements, but apparently he considered it an experiment. It was his first attempt at an imperial mosque on a grand scale so he increased its size by adding four semi-domes around a large central dome. To make this structurally viable four solid supports had to be inserted into the main hall. Sinan felt they looked clumsy and out of place inside the vast interior, and never used this same layout again.

The rather stark interior is a foil for the detail laden courtyard, two minarets and the exterior of the dome and semi domes. Seen in silhouette, fretted cornices form a line atop the structure with ribbing and colonnaded galleries providing interest through an array of repetition and contrast. On hot days it's very pleasant to walk around the back where you'll find seats shaded by stately Cypress trees.

Address: Main entry on Şehzadebaşı Caddesi in section of street since renamed 15 Temmuz Şehitleri Caddesi in reference to the attempted coup in 2016.

Catch a 336E, 35, 78, 93, 97GE or 146B from the Eminönü bus terminal and alight at İstanbul Büyükşehir Belediyesi stop. At the intersection cross the road to the left so you're heading towards a park on the corner. Be really careful when you cross and look everywhere, even when you have the green walk sign. There's an entry about 200m along where the park ends or you can continue further along and enter by the main gate. It's nearest to the tombs.

HALİÇ
Both sides of the Golden Horn

Abraham Salomon Kamondo Anıt Mezarı

It's likely every visitor to Istanbul has heard of the Camondo Stairs in Galata, even if they haven't visited them. This undulating staircase flowing organically from a central axis is a fusion of Neo-Baroque and early Art Nouveau design built in the late 19th century. Far less well known is the Kamondo Anıt Mezarı, the tomb of Abraham Salomon de Camondo, the man who ordered their construction. Abraham Camondo was born in Constantinople sometime between 1781 and 1785. The de Camondo, a name that means Casa de Mondo or House of the World in Spanish, were Sephardic Jews who'd been expelled from the Iberian Peninsula in 1492. Originally they'd settled in Trieste when it was ruled by the Venetians, but after the Austrians took over in 1798 they came to Turkey.

Through his bank and other connections, Abraham Camondo provided money to aid the Ottoman Empire during the Crimean War of 1853 to 1855, partnered with cargo shipping companies and funded tramways. He also helped modernise Constantinople when the very first Istanbul municipal council, called the Altıncı Daire-i Belediye, the Sixth Department of Istanbul, was established. He and the rest of the Camondo family were also known for their philanthropic activities in the Jewish communities of the city. However, when

164

the Ottoman state changed their policies concerning international and domestic economic strategies, Abraham Camondo moved to Paris.

Abraham died one year later in 1873. He'd always planned to be buried in Istanbul and when his body was returned a state ceremony was held. According to accounts of the day, it was a solemn and grand occasion, reflecting how loved and respected Camondo was. Sultan Abdülhamid II attended, the stock market and banks were closed, and traders and shopkeepers pulled down their shutters as church bells rang out while Abraham Salmon was laid to rest.

His mausoleum stands forlornly on a hill above the D100 highway stretching across the Golden Horn. You'll see it just behind the sign to the large recycling facility next door. The tomb itself bears no markers or historical explanations. Judging by the piles of bones on the ground stripped of any meat, stray dogs are the only frequent visitors. They growl when you approach but quickly move away and soon ignore you. Just stay calm and walk slowly.

These days the site is really rather bleak, but it's easy to imagine what it must have been like when Abraham Camondo made his last journey home. Rolling green hills would have covered the place where the highway was built, with small wooden houses, mosques and synagogues reaching down to the banks of the estuary. You can still get a glimpse of old Istanbul if you walk over the road that crosses the highway and walk up a small street perpendicular to it. There's a huge active cemetery on the left and a smaller, seemingly neglected one on the right. Looks can be deceiving. It's actually a Jewish cemetery and descendants of the occupants still visit to lay flowers and pray. Follow the road further along and you'll find yourself in Çıksalın. It's a less well-off neighbourhood of Istanbul where people go about their everyday business. Many are from Erzincan and run Tandir Evi, small food establishments producing bread and other items in tandoor ovens.

Address: Beyoğlu Belediye Başkanlığı No 20, Sütlüce

The easiest way to get to the tomb is to catch a Metrobus to Halıçoğlu. Metrobuses start in Kadıköy on the Asian side or you can pick one up in Zeytinburnu on the European side. When you alight at the Halıçoğlu stop walk away from the water, climb the stairs to the overpass and turn left. The tomb is about a 10-minute walk from there. You can go back the same way but if you decide to meander through Çıksalın and have lunch, you can catch a 54HT from down in Hasköy Square to the Şişhane 2 stop. From Şişhane 2 you can walk up to Istiklal Caddesi in about 10 minutes. Alternatively, stay on a few stops longer and you can get out in the Taksim tunnel and go upstairs to the square.

Aynalıkavak Kasrı

Set in a peaceful, well-laid out formal garden overlooking the Golden Horn, Aynalıkavak Kasrı is one of the many buildings that previously made up the grand Aynalıkavak Palace. The palace was built during the time of Sultan Ahmet III (1703-1730). Translated, Aynalıkavak is the Palace of the Mirrored Poplars, in reference to a set of large mirrors sent to Sultan Ahmet III as a gift after the Ottoman-Venetian War of 1714-1718. It's also known as the 'shipyard palace' because it overlooks the site of the historic 15th Century Haliç Tersanesi, the Golden Horn shipyards, established by Sultan Mehmet II (Mehmet the Conqueror) in 1453.

At one time Aynalıkavak was the fourth largest palace in Istanbul, after Dolmabahçe, Topkapı and Üsküdar palaces. Largely overlooked today, it was here representatives of the Turkish and Russian governments met to hammer out the details of the Aynalıkavak Treaty, originally signed in Kuchuk Kainardji (present-day Bulgaria) in 1774. Certain clauses in the initial agreement regarding the treatment of Ottoman Christians and Crimean Tatars needed clarification and a meeting in the palace on March 10, 1779 rectified that.

Today, all that remains of the complex is Aynalıkavak Kasrı, a pavilion or summer palace, sometimes also referred to as the Imperial Garden Pavilion. It's set on a narrow extremely busy road but the minute you pass through the gates the noise fades away. Although modest in size, Aynalıkavak Kasrı is an exquisite example of late Ottoman architecture that owes its present state to repairs and alternations undertaken by Sultan Selim III (1789-1807).

I went there with a Turkish girlfriend. After paying the entry fees the same security guard who'd taken our money escorted us to the building. It's covered in a metal clad roof with a small dome, eaves and a long overhang protecting a grand doorway where the guard waited as we put on our plastic shoe covers. Then he carefully showed us how to use the audio guides. Well just me actually, because I'm hopeless with them.

The main door opens onto an anteroom and through to five more rooms. In the Divanhane, which sits under the dome, Sultan Selim III's *tuğra* takes pride of place in the ceiling decorations. Tuğra are the Ottoman equivalent of a royal monogram, elaborate calligraphy signatures that are as ornamental as they are authoritative. His flows beautifully and is covered in gold leaf. There's a 54 couplet poem about the pavilion engraved on the arch windows, while in the *hasoda*, or privy chamber, the windows are decorated with a 36 couplet poem by Sheikh Galib. The work was completed by calligrapher Yesârîzâde Mustafa İzzet Efendi.

The security guard waited patiently as we took our time gazing at the interior and marvelled at the exquisitely hand-painted wall panels, lush furnishings and serene views over the gardens. The lighting was extraordinary inside, partly due to the number of windows, but also through the use of glass pieces inserted into plaster carvings near the ceiling. Every surface was covered in a different type of material, carved wood, brocaded cloth, gilded finishes, etched symbols and elaborate patterns, all designed to reflect the light and increase delight.

The audio guide is extremely informative and descriptive. It's easy to identity what you're looking at so learning what the many decorative features signify more than makes up for not being allowed to take photographs. Consequently, by the time we got to the small but very detailed Music Museum in the basement floor I was on sensory and information overload. In a good way though. I enjoyed learning that Sultan Selim III's engaged with his artistic side by composing and performing music but must confess I skipped rather quickly past most of the displays on the lower floor. I did stop to inspect particularly exquisite or more unusual instruments but as a big fan of ethnology museums, no matter how small, I've already seen similar displays pertaining to music history elsewhere in Turkey.

Address: Donanma Caddesi, Keçeci Piri, Hasköy

The easiest way to get there from the Eminönü bus terminal is to catch bus numbers 47E, 47C 50E and alight at Aynalıkavak. From Taksim catch the 36T, 38T or 54HT and get off at the same stop. The entrance gate is around 30 metres back in the direction you've come from. You can also catch the Haliç (Golden Horn) Şehir ferry and walk up from the Hasköy Wharf in about 15 minutes but having done it I don't recommend it unless you're a fan of traffic.

Opening times: 09.00-18.00, Tue-Sun. Closed Mondays. Last tickets sold 17.30.

Entry fee: free with Museum Card, otherwise 40tl or 10tl for garden only where there's a cafe serving tea, coffee, light snacks and Turkish breakfasts.

Küçük Mustafa Paşa Hamamı

The name of this hamam translates as the Little Mustafa Pasha Turkish bath but it was constructed by one Kara Mustafa Paşa in 1477, during the reign of Fatih Sultan Mehmet, the Mehmet the Conqueror who took Byzantium in 1453. Kara, or Koca Mustafa Paşa as he was also referred to, went on to become the Grand Vizier to Sultan Beyazit II. Beyazit II ruled from 1481 to 1512 and as his Grand Vizier, Mustafa Paşa would have had enormous power over political decisions, finance and military campaigns. Given the *camekan*, at 14.5 metres square, is among the largest changing areas in any of the hamam in the city, including the word small in the name seems something of a misnomer.

This 15th century hamam, one of the largest in Istanbul, was originally divided into two sections for men and women. The domed camekan had upper floors built from wood where men would change before and after their baths while the lower floor was used as an area to relax and cool down. In some of the smaller rooms originally used to sweat out impurities, the underfloor section is visible, showing how hot water would flow throughout the whole structure and create steam. In addition to its sheer

170

size, the Küçük Mustafa Paşa Hamamı is impressive due to the intricately carved stalactites inside the central dome of the *hararet*, the heat chamber and the juxtaposition of different sizes and styles of brickwork and coloured marble throughout.

Address: Müstantik Caddesi No 32, Cibali

Catch a 36CE, 44B, 44E, 99, 99A or 99Y bus from the Eminönü bus terminal to the Ayakapı stop. After you get off back track slightly and turn right onto Miralay Nazımbey Caddesi. Follow it until you see Küçük Mustafa Paşa Caddesi. Turn left and then turn left at the intersection with Şerifiye Sokak. The entrance to the building is about 20 metres down on the right.

Opening times: Küçük Mustafa Paşa Hamamı is currently used as an exhibition space so you'll need to check in advance to see what's on and when you can visit.

Sveti Stefan Kilesi

For many of the years I've lived in Istanbul, the pale green grey cast iron Bulgarian Church, or Saint Stephen of the Bulgars to give its full name, had been closed. I'd glide past it on a ferry on my way further up the Haliç waterway and wonder if it was worth the crawlingly slow bus trip along the traffic clogged coastal road to see it up close from land, if only from the outside. Provided, that is, I was able to find the caretaker and convince him to let me in. This being Istanbul, there was always something else to take my fancy so I didn't get there until it reopened in 2018.

The church now standing on the shores of the Golden Horn was first opened for worship on September 8, 1898. It replaced the original Saint Stephen of the Bulgars church, a simple structure made of wood erected in the early 19th century when the Bulgarian Church was trying to break away from the Greek Orthodox Patriarchate of Istanbul. At the time the Ecumenical Patriarch of Constantinople controlled all the religious affairs of Orthodox congregations throughout the entire Eastern Christian world. This meant the Bulgarians had to worship at Greek Orthodox churches but they wanted somewhere to call their own. Bulgarian nationalists agitated for change and they were finally granted permission to have their own Exarchate, that is a bishop with control over the Bulgarian diocese in Istanbul.

Like many buildings in Istanbul in previous centuries, the wooden St Stephen's was severely damaged in a fire, so a decision was made to erect a church constructed entirely of iron. Istanbul born Armenian architect Hovsep Aznavur was chosen to draw up the construction plans and a competition held to find the best company to produce the prefabricated steel parts to be used in the structure. The winners, an Austrian company called R Ph Waagner Vienne, used neo-Gothic and neo-Baroque styles and cast each section piece-by-piece in Vienna between 1893 and 1896. Founded by Rudolph Philipp Waagner in 1854, the company is still in the business of steel and mechanical engineering under the name Waagner Biro.

On completion, everything was loaded onto a boat that travelled down the Danube and arrived in Istanbul via the Black Sea. Somewhat like a giant Meccano set, it took one and a half years to put all the pieces together. The final product had three domes set atop a cross shaped basilica where the congregation could worship, with a 40-metre-high belfry set above the narthex. Bells cast in Yaroslavl, a city northeast of Moscow, rang out over the water, calling the devout to prayer. Over the ensuing years the church fell into disrepair. Its future was uncertain until a 2011 agreement between Bulgaria and Turkey saw the start of extensive renovation work.

It was reinaugurated as an official place of worship on January 8, 2018, the 120th anniversary of the iron church.

On an overcast day the exterior almost blends with the sky but whatever the weather, the interior is a blaze of gold. Once your eyes adjust, have a closer look at the panels on the revetments, the retaining walls. They look like they're made of marble but are in fact cast iron that echo when you knock. If the staircases to the upper gallery are open go up and gaze over at the gleaming, decorative portraits lined up along the gold-framed iconostasis. Ignore the wannabe Instagrammers that compete for attention and instead soak up the riches of the gilded panels of the arched ceiling overhead. On your way out

Saint Stephen of the Bulgars Church at sunset

look for the swirling palm fronds emerging from
Corinthian column head designed iron window grills
and take a turn through the grounds to pay your
respects before the graves of former metropolitans
of the Bulgarian Church.

Address: Mürselpaşa Caddesi in a park between the
Fener ferry wharf and the Balat tram stop.

Sveti Stefan Kilesi was built at a time when prefabricated iron churches were being put up all over
the world but today it's one of the few still in
existence. A nice way to get to it is to catch a city
line ferry from Eminönü and disembark at Fener.

This is an ordinary ferry you can take and pay for with your Istanbul Card. Head for the wharf called Haliç Şehir Hat and politely ignore the touts offering more expensive tours up the Golden Horn, unless you're interested in one of course. When you disembark head straight up to the road running parallel to the Golden Horn. Once there turn right. The church is a three-minute walk.

Alternatively, catch the Eminönü-Alibey tram from the Eminönü transport hub and get off at Balat. Turn and start back the way you've come. Keep the water on your left and when it's safe, cross the road and cut through the park that divides the traffic heading in different directions. Head for the parallel road on the other side of the park and keep heading in the same direction as when you got off the tram. The church is around a five-minute walk from the tram stop.

Opening times: 09.00-17.00, 7 days a week

Tekfur Sarayı Müzesi

Built partially within Istanbul's *sur*, the old city walls, Tekfur Sarayı, the Palace of the Sovereign, was named for the 10th century emperor Constantine VII Porphyrogenitus. It's also known as the Palace of the Porphyrogenitus but no one has been able to ascertain the exact date it was built or by whom. It most likely dates to the late 13th or possible the early 14th century and was built as an annex to the larger Blachernae Palace, a complex used by Byzantine emperors from the beginning of the 12th century.

Tekfur Sarayı is a three-storey building with four large arches on the ground floor, set in front of a courtyard containing auxiliary buildings around the periphery. There are five huge windows on the first floor and seven smaller ones on the floor above. The ground floor arches are picked out in white stone while the windows on the two floors above feature a distinctive red and white pattern on their curves. The exterior wall is made up of horizontal stripes in the two colours, stretching across its width.

During the 16th and 17th centuries Tekfur Sarayı housed a menagerie, a type of zoo, where visitors could marvel at large exotic animals such

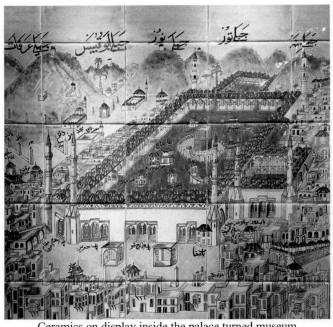

Ceramics on display inside the palace turned museum

as elephants and giraffes. By the end of that time the animals had been moved elsewhere and the building functioned as a brothel, although only for a short while. Equally fascinating but far less certain is the rumour the *Kaşıkçı Elması*, the Spoonmaker's Diamond, was found in rubbish on the grounds of the palace in 1669. This 86-carat (12.2g) pear-shaped diamond is on display at Topkapı Palace.

In 1719 a glass and ceramics workshop was established on the premises, mainly producing what were known as Tekfur Sarayı tiles. They were lesser in quality than those produced in Iznik but their pretty designs showing European influence made them much sought after. By the second half of the eighteenth century their popularity was in decline and the project petered out. The structure fell into decay, losing its roof and parts of the floors. Nonetheless it served as a poor house for Istanbul Jews at the beginning of the 19th century, and glass continued to be produced here until 1920. After that it was in turns a workshop and depot, but eventually the once grand Palace of the Porphyrogenitus was reduced to only the four main walls with their distinctive red and white stone blocks and a few facings of white marble set out in geometrical patterns. Nothing else of the Blachernae Palace complex remained.

The building underwent reconstruction from 1955 to 1970 and then again more recently, starting from around 2006, before being completed in 2019. Tekfur Sarayı is now open as a museum containing detailed and beautiful displays showcasing an extensive range of ceramic, glass and crockery items. They range from everyday pots, bowls and pipe heads made from clay to delicate coffee cups and tile panels depicting cityscapes. The most stunning item on display in my opinion is a ceramic *mihrab*, the Muslim prayer niche, relocated in its entirety from an Istanbul mosque. It's the first thing you see at the very top of the final flight of stairs and demands close attention. That said, if views are your thing, continue on up the next flight of stairs out into the fresh air. The flat roof has been converted into a viewing platform from where you can see all the way up the Golden Horn, look over at Pera and Galata Tower and gaze at the tankers and ferries making their way up the Bosphorus.

Address: Şişhane Caddesi, Ayvansaray, Fatih

Getting to the palace depends on where you start from. I always catch a bus from the Eminönü bus terminal. You can take a 336E, 36KE, 37E, 38E and get off at the Edirnekapı Surdışı stop. From there it's about a 10-minute walk. I suggest you screenshot the walk from the bus stop to the museum before you set off. You can either return the same way or slowly wend your way down the hill to the neighbourhood of Balat. From there you can catch a ferry or bus back to Eminönü. I generally avoid the buses because they're usually packed and the traffic is horrific so you can be stuck for some time. The Eminönü-Alibey tram is preferable.

You can also get to this museum using the Eminönü-Alibey tram from the Eminönü transport hub. Get off at Balat then turn right and walk along Ayvansaray Caddesi, the road running parallel to the water, next to the park. When you come to the point where the two sides of the road meet (as in, it's no longer a divided road), turn left and walk up Çınçınlı Çeşme Sokak. From here the walk up to the palace takes about 15 minutes. It's twists and turns a bit at the end so I suggest you screenshot the route before you head out.

Opening times: 10.00-17.00, Tue-Sun. Closed Mondays. Entry fee 24tl.

Vlaherna Meryem Ana Kilisesi

When Istanbul was Constantinople, neighbourhoods in the northwestern section of the city along Haliç, the Golden Horn, were home to numerous prominent churches. The most important was and is the Aya Yorgi Rum Kilisesi ve Fener Rum Patrikhanesi, Saint George's Church and Ecumenical Patriarchate, the seat of the Eastern Orthodox Church. However there were dozens of other religious sites including the Vlaherna Meryem Ana Kilisesi.

Blakernai, to give Vlaherna its Greek name, was a district famous for a holy spring, called *hagiasma* in Greek and *ayazma* in Turkish. The Blakernai holy spring was named for Meryem Ana, that is Mother Mary as in Mary Magdalene, the mother of Jesus, who many believed changed the course of battle when the Avars from the North Caucasus region besieged Constantinople in 626AD. With the enemy at the gates, the Greek Patriarch Sergios stood aloft the walls, holding up a painting of the Virgin Mary. He called on all believers to pray to her. While it's unlikely divine intervention was the reason the Avars failed to take the city, hundreds of people were convinced they saw the Virgin Mary striding along the city walls, sword in hand, smoting down the enemy.

The Church of the Virgin Mary, the Panagia Blacherniotissa, was built by Empress Pulcheria in about 450AD. She was the sister of Theodosius II, of underground cistern fame. It was later expanded by Emperor Leo I and renovated by Justinian I in the 6th century. The plain, almost pedestrian structure that awaits at the end of a long path through unexpectedly pretty gardens (the surrounding buildings are less than salubrious) gives nothing away. Inside, the church and *ayazma* are housed in a single rectangular room. Wooden seats line one wall opposite the marble facade built over the spring, while an iconostasis with four panels and a central door takes up the adjoining space. Indoor photography is forbidden but even if that weren't the case, I don't think photos could translate the sombre atmosphere. Vlaherna Meryem Ana has all the similar religious accoutrements of other Orthodox churches I've entered, flickering candles, the scent of incense, gold leaf everything, but feels sadder in some way. Maybe it's because there was no service in progress when I was there, so the past and what's been lost, both in my life and those of members of the church, were more prominent in my thoughts than the present.

Address: Ayvansaray Kuyusu Sokak, Ayvansaray

The most scenic way to get there is to catch the Haliç Şehir Hat, the Golden Horn city line ferry that stops near the Eminönü bus terminal and disembark at Ayvansaray. Ignore touts offering Bosphorus and other tours, and click thought the turnstiles with your Istanbul Card. Walk from the wharf to the Ayvansaray tram stop then use the directions in the next paragraph.

You can also catch the Eminönü-Alibey tram from the Eminönü transport hub and get off at Ayvansaray. You'll be on Ayvansaray Caddesi, the main road running along the Golden Horn. Head for the traffic lights. The road opposite is Ayvansaray Kuyusu Sokağı. There's a large stone wall on the right-hand side of the street and a fountain on the left. Walk straight along it until you come to a V intersection. The entrance to the church is directly opposite. The church is a little over a 5-minute walk from both the ferry wharf and the tram stop.

Opening times: 09.00-17.00, 7 days a week

KARAKÖY

Schneidertempel Sanat Merkezi

The majority of tourists who come to Galata head straight for the tower and if they have time, explore the steep and narrow backstreets full of stylish boutique hotels, upmarket cafes and shops selling unique and whimsical souvenirs. The area has a cosmopolitan feel. That's largely due to the mix of people you'll come across at any given moment, chatting in Italian, whispering in French, talking in Spanish and laughing in Arabic.

I'm talking about 21st century Galata but the scene I've just described could have been any time in the last several hundred years. Traders from Genoa, Arabs from Andalusia, local born Rum and Armenians to name a few, have all called the neighbourhood home at one point or another. Many of them are long dead while others have moved on. Often all that's left are architectural traces such as the Schneidertempel Art Gallery.

At street level, the entryway to this gallery appears no different from many other doorways in the area, until you put your head back and look up. The clue is on the lintel, where an inscription in Hebrew reading "For my house will be called a house of prayer for all peoples" indicates its past. The Schneidertempel Art Gallery was once the Shneyder Temple, the Tailors' Synagogue. While Islam was the predominant religion during the Ottoman Empire, different religious groups were allowed a significant degree of autonomy over their own communities. This became more formalised in the 18th century through the *millet* system when the Ottoman Empire began to divide its citizenry into millet. Each millet consisted of a different religion and they were free to practice their beliefs which is how synagogues like this one and other non-Muslim places of worship exist in Istanbul today.

A guild of Ashkenazi Jews commissioned the construction and the Shneyder Temple opened for worship on September 8, 1894. As the name indicates, the congregation was made up of tailors, the majority from the Russian territories, working in Galata. Just over a hundred years later the number of worshippers had dropped so much the remaining community members decided to convert the synagogue into a gallery. It opened in 1998 with the interior left untouched. There's a coloured glass Star of David above the *bimah,* literally the desk where the Rabbi would speak and assorted items from when the synagogue was still active. A chair used by a sculptor named Fogelstein gleams with polish and a small collection of objects, photos and postcards showing the life and pastimes of the community are on display along the upper tiers.
Address: Felek Sokak No1, Karaköy

From Galata Tower head down to Bereketzade Medresesi Sokak. Felek Sokak is a small street on the left just before you reach the Camondo Staircase. If you're coming from Karaköy ferry wharf head for the stairs and ascend. Felek Sok is at the top, to the right.

Opening times: 11.00-18.00, Tue-Sun. Closed Mondays. Free entry.

Yeraltı Camii

When my Dad came to visit me in Istanbul in 2007 I went inside more mosques than I can remember. He was fascinated by them, so much so he'd happily slip a pair of women's *şalvar*, traditional voluminous baggy pants, or an elastic waisted floral cotton skirt over the sturdy King Gee shorts he always wore when he travelled. It didn't matter if the interior was highly elaborate or simple and understated, in the week he was here I often had to rescue him from being run over by taxis and trams when he suddenly dashed across the road in pursuit of fulfilling his single-minded obsession.

This being Istanbul a life time wouldn't be long enough to see every mosque in the city. Unless you set out to visit one every day, but even then I'm not sure. Luckily Yeraltı Camii is easy to get to. The exterior won't make you think there's anything particularly exciting about it, until you know the history of this subterranean space converted into a mosque by Grand Vizier Bahir Mustafa Paşa in 1757. First the architectural details. Inside there are 54 thick squat columns arranged in neat lines and the only natural light source comes from windows in the wall on the sea side so the mosque is cold underfoot, no matter the time of year. The original minaret was destroyed in an earthquake and a replacement commissioned by Sultan Mahmud.

Yeraltı Mosque interior

When Galata was a Genoese settlement the site
where the mosque now stands was in the basement
of a Byzantine fort, the Kastellion Tower. The
carpeted area where worshippers now pray was the
storage area of the enormous long chain strung
across the waterway to stop Turkish fleets from
entering the Golden Horn and attacking the city.
When Constantinople finally fell to the Ottomans in
1453 the site became an ammunition dump.
However the mosque has an even earlier history
although that wasn't discovered until sometime
later.

Yeraltı Camii is also known as Kurşunlumahzen
Camii and gets its importance from the people
buried there. In 1640 a Sufi dervish of the
Nakşibendi sect is said to have seen the grave of
Süfyan bin Uyeyne in a dream. Süfyan bin Uyeyne

185

was one of the companions of the Prophet Muhammad, and fought with him during the first Arab siege of Constantinople that took place from 674 to 687AD. He was captured during the siege and held prisoner in the dungeon, ultimately dying of starvation. When the Sufi looked in the place he'd seen in his vision, he found the graves of bin Uyeyne and another martyred Arab soldier, Vehb bin Hüseyre. The tombs of these two Islamic martyrs are at rear of the mosque when you enter from the sea doors, in a gated room bathed in green light. Yeraltı is particularly busy during the month of Ramazan when people traditionally come to pray and offer supplications at the tombs.

However Karaköy is always busy with lots of people from all over the place and signs outside the mosque advise you not to leave your shoes outside when you enter, just in case they aren't there when you come back out. I always carry a spare shopping bag in whatever handbag or day pack I'm using so I can take mine in with me and not have to worry about them.

Address: Kemankeş Caddesi No 23, Karamustafa Paşa, Karaköy

The mosque is located one street back from the waterfront in Karaköy, a minute's walk from the large Şehir Hat ferry wharf.

SEA OF MARMARA AND NEARBY NEIGHBOURHOODS

Balıklı Meryem Ana Rum Ortadoks Manıstırı

Recognised as the Monastery of the Life-Giving Spring by Google, I much prefer the literal name Mother Mary Greek Orthodox Church of the Fishes (or 'with Fishes', to be exact). Situated in the midst of a large cemetery shaded by tall trees and thick shrubbery, with different sections dedicated to Turkish, Rum and Armenian graves, this monastery is a 10-minute walk along a road opposite Silivrikapı (Silivri Gate), part of the original city walls dating back to the 5th century AD.

You access the monastery by walking through large wooden double entry doors that lead into a simple courtyard. In the heat of the midday sun, on my first visit here, everything was glaringly white, even the trunk of the huge plane tree cut short, but still throwing a measure of shade with its thriving branches, over on one side. The church was officially closed to visitors due to the Coronavirus pandemic (don't worry, it's open again now) but I spied a man in an office and asked very nicely, in Turkish, if we could go inside. Smilingly he said yes and picked up a really huge key (it was about a foot long) and led us to the narthex. We carefully stepped inside over the marble step and watched as he slowly inserted the key into the lock and let us in.

Inside the layout is typical of Orthodox churches, however there's a triple nave with an elaborate and quite beautiful iconostasis at the rear and a luminous shell shaped pulpit winding its way towards the heavens on the left. The iconostasis is decorated with scenes from the life of Jesus Christ with a depiction of the Last Supper in the pediment, the triangular bit on top. At eye level there's a portrait of Mary and the baby Jesus, saints such as Theodora, Demetrios and Nikolaos, as well as the Archangels Michael and Gabriel. More scenes cover the opposite end of the nave including the Expulsion of Adam and Eve from Paradise and religious portraits on the pediment itself. I'm not at all religious but the beauty and attention to detail of churches like these caress my soul.

The church was originally named Zoodohos Piyi, meaning bestower or source of life, after the *ayazma*, a sacred underground water source located next to it. According to legend, when Justinianus I was still a young man and not yet Byzantine Emperor and therefore leader of the eastern world, he was wandering around the area one day when a blind old man approached him. The man asked Justinianus to take him to a water source. Justinianus looked everywhere but couldn't locate any water until a holy voice told him where to find it. The voice told him if the blind man washed his face with this water, he'd regain his sight. It also told Justinianus that if he drank from the water, he'd become an emperor. When this came about in 457 AD, Justinianus gave orders for a structure to be built over the sacred water source, and also a church.

A thousand years later the complex had become known as the Balıklı Meryen Ana Rum Manastırı. The name comes from a story concerning a man frying fish beside the sacred source in the year 1453 AD. While he was cooking the fish someone came around and announced the Turks had conquered the city. Incredulous, the man said he believed the news as much as he believed the fish could be resurrected. Suddenly the fish came back to life, jumped into the sacred pool and started swimming again.

Whatever the truth of the matter the water in the ayazma is a startlingly clear aquamarine and although I didn't notice any fish, alive or otherwise, I'm living proof it is potable. I had a taste using one of the aluminium cups provided. Written notices invite you to take one of the small plastic bottles filled with water lined up on the steps should you so wish. They're free of charge. I think they're best left for believers but it's up to you. At certain times of the year special services are held down here and small icons and biblical scenes adorn some of the walls and arches. The path to the ayazma is down a flight of stairs, accessed through a small graveyard with tombs of some of the church patriarchs.

In the courtyard where you first enter, the ground is paved with headstones. Some sources say they were brought here from cemeteries elsewhere in the city to be protected from destruction. Whatever the case, they have fascinating symbols and carvings depicting the professions of the deceased on them. My husband and I and a couple of Turkish women took delight in trying to work out who was what and managed to identify a number of farmers (or possibly land owners), an architect and a grocer, to name a few. At first glance I thought the script was Greek, but it turned out to be Karamanlı Turkish. Karamanlides people lived in Anatolia. One theory has them as a Turkified Greek-speaking Byzantine population while another claims they were originally soldiers placed in central Turkey by Byzantine emperors, retaining their language and Orthodox religion. Either way, they wrote in Turkish using the Greek alphabet, which meant none of us could read the words. When the 1923 population exchange took place, enabled by the League of Nations, the Karamanlı were some of the 1.2 million Turkish born Greeks forcibly sent to Greece, in exchange for some 350-400,000 Greek born Turks moved to Turkey in exchange. Today little of their history remains, making these gravestones even more poignant.

Much like the small shrine created in the hollow trunk of the plane tree. You have to walk around the back of the tree to see it. Inside the narrow vertical opening there's a hanging lamp, icon and candle.

Address: Balıklı Silivrikapı Sokak, Seyitnizam, Zeytinburnu

How you get there depends on where you start from, but I caught the Marmaray to the Kazlıçeşme stop. From there a 48A bus leaves every ten minutes and it's only 7 stops to the Silivrikapı bus stop where you need to alight. The A10 and 85C buses also pass this stop but run less frequently. Cross the road and walk down Seyit Nizam Caddesi almost directly opposite. This leads through the cemetery. At the Y intersection 100 metres in, veer right then continue straight until you reach the entry to the monastery through a low door on your left.

Opening times: 08.30-16.30, 7 days a week

Türkiye Ermenileri Patrikliği

The grand, two storey wooden Armenian Patriarchate of Constantinople building is tucked down a backstreet in a poor and ramshackle neighbourhood populated by displaced people, both legal and not, from all corners of the globe. Until 1461 it was located in Bursa. That's where prelate Archbishop Hovageem (Joachim), the ecclesiastical head of the church, lived and worked. After Fatih Sultan Mehmet rode into town in 1453 and took over, he ordered all Armenians move to the newly conquered city of Constantinople, now modern-day Istanbul. Archbishop Hovageem became the spiritual head of the Armenians under the rule of the Sultan, better known as Mehmet the Conqueror.

The original Patriarchate was built on land granted to the church in Samatya, but in 1641 they moved a few suburbs east to Kumpkapı. The location of the actual patriarchate is on a block opposite the site of the Surp Vortvots Vorodman Church. The name translates as "The Children of the Thunder" and this place of worship dates back to Byzantine times.

An impressive complex has been built around it. The main church is the Holy Asdvadzadzin (Virgin Mary) Armenian Church which is now the official seat of the Armenian Patriarchate of Constantinople. A see or seat is the bishop's area of ecclesiastical jurisdiction, and the patriarchate is the administrative centre. The Holy Asdvadzadzin Church was actually planned as three churches next to each other. The Children of the Thunder or simply the South Church was blessed as Holy Hagop (the Holy Vortvots Vorodman) and the North as Holy Sarkis. This latter church is also known as the Outside Church and functions as a place of worship for Ethiopian Christians living in Istanbul. In the crypt there's an *ayazma,* a holy spring dedicated to Saint Theodore, but it's not often open to the public. Compared to others I've seen it's fairly basic, just a small tap over a marble basin set into the wall. If you ask at the front gate the caretaker might let you in to fill your bottle. There's also a large hall, home to the Mesrob Mutafyan Culture Centre and the private Bezciyan Armenian School in separate grounds next door.

The Virgin Mary church has been damaged and restored many times in its history. On the 6th of July 1718 it's believed there was a huge fire lasting thirty hours. Fifty thousand houses went up in flames and fifteen people died. The rebuilt church was blessed in 1719 and over time became known as the Main Church. It was again badly damaged on the 17th of May, in 1762, and repaired in 1764 with the help of the Archbishop Hagop Nalyan (1706-1764), a famous theologian and poet, along with his close friend the Grand Vizier Koca Ragıp Pasa (1669-1763). Despite further fires the church has been in continuous active use since 1828. Its present state is the work of Krikor Amira Balyan, a member of the eminent Balyan family of architects.

It's a popular location for weddings and if you're lucky you might see gaggles of little girls running around in acres of tulle playing fairies, solemn little boys dressed in black bow ties and long trousers, and dignified young women bedecked in elegant white wedding dresses.

Address: Sevgi Sokak No 3, Muhsine Hatun, Kumkapı

Getting to the Armenian Patriarchate very much depends where you are staying. It's a 10-minute walk from Yenkapı Marmaray or 20 minutes on foot from Sultanahmet Square. Otherwise take the tram from Sultanahmet heading to Bağcılar and get out at the Beyazıt/Kapalıçarşı stop, then walk 10 minutes down hill through narrow streets full of wholesale traders. I suggest you Google and then screenshot the route before you set off. There are a lot of people from all over the world passing through this area so be alert to who's around you, and keep your valuables in sight. Commonsense suggests you don't visit at night as it is very deserted in some parts and less than salubrious in others.

Opening times: the Churches are open for services on Sundays, Orthodox Easter and Christmas. You're welcome to access the grounds and enter partway into the Holy Asdvadzadzin Armenian Church on other days of the week.

Florya Atatürk Deniz Köşkü

Today the European shores of the Sea of Marmara are a mix of overly built-up suburbs and kilometres of walking, cycling and skating paths. However, in the first half of the 20th century they were the site of sea hamam, where respectable women and children could swim curtained off from the prying eyes of men, who'd much rather enjoy the entertainments on offer in *gazino*, the Turkish version of nightclubs often featuring live music and dancing.

Walkway to the Florya Atatürk Sea Pavilion

In 1921, a trio of refugees living in Istanbul consisting of a Russian prince, count and colonel, leased an abandoned beach site near Florya, did it up and opened for business as a beach resort. In a nod to changing times they allowed mixed bathing so it's probably no coincidence Florya is where Mustafa Kemal Atatürk, the founder of the modern Turkish Republic, ordered Istanbul's first public beach opened in 1932.

Atatürk liked the area so much he had a summer house built in the Bauhaus Style, in 1935. Now known as the Florya Atatürk Deniz Köşkü, this former private residence sits 70 metres out to sea above the Sea of Marmara. Designed by architect Seyfi Arkan, the building was completed on August 14 and given to Atatürk by the then mayor of Istanbul. A long boardwalk leads to the pavilion, itself built on steel columns driven into the sea bed.

Inside the rooms are just as Atatürk would have had them, filled with some truly wonderful examples of Bauhaus furniture and the great man's personal memorabilia. It gives much more of an insight into Atatürk at ease rather than the man of action like in other museums of his I've visited. There's even a pair of Atatürk's swimming trunks on display and photos of him enjoying himself in summer. Photos dating to 1936 show Atatürk, a keen swimmer and rower, enjoying himself at Solaryum Beach while his adoring public looked on.

Address: Çekmece Istanbul Caddesi No 23, Florya, Bakırköy

When I first lived in Istanbul in 2000, getting anywhere in the city took a very long time. Now all you have to do is catch the Marmaray from Sirkeci station and get out at Florya station. Even from where I live, in Göztepe, on the other side of the city, the journey only takes 50 minutes from my door to the entry way of the pavilion, including the walk from Florya station to the pavilion. At Florya station take the exit facing the water, turn right and walk 300 metres along Çekmece İstanbul Caddesi with the water on your left. You'll come to a street veering down to the left with a low gate at the entryway and a sign reading TBMM Florya Sosyal Tesisleri. Walk through the grounds until you come to the ticket booth for the museum.

Just make sure the train you take has Halkalı as its final destination, otherwise you'll have to get off and wait again.

Opening times: 09.00-17.00, Tue–Sun. Closed Mondays. Entry fee 20tl.

TAKSIM

Ali Muhiddin Hacı Bekir

See page 32 for more information

Address: İstiklal Caddesi No 83/A, Beyoğlu (just down from Taksim).

Meryem Ana Rum Ortodoks Kilisesi

Dedicated to the Virgin Mary, this Greek Orthodox Church is the oldest church in the district of Beyoğlu, formerly known as Pera. It was designed by architect Hacı Komninos Kalfa with permission from Sultan Selim III and opened on 18 September 1804.

Located up a short lane way off Istiklal Caddesi you'll never see it unless you're looking for it. I passed it dozens of times before I realised there was a building behind the steel fence at the end. After that, whenever I checked, the gates were always locked, even though there's a sign on the wall advertising daily opening hours.

One day I saw two women being admitted into the grounds and quickly ran after them. I found them sitting on a bench seat at the top of a short flight of stairs, outside a building opposite a large basilica. We got chatting and it turned out they were visiting from Greece and when I told them how many times I'd tried to see the interior of the church, they were more than happy for me to tag along. A few minutes later the custodian appeared with a big ring of keys. He was a little taken aback to see me with them but as soon as I started to chat in Turkish he relaxed and led the three of us around to the main entry door.

Ceiling details in the narthex of the Virgin Mary Greek Orthodox Church

Like all the Orthodox churches I've visited in Istanbul the key to open the door is enormous but he handled it with flair.

Entry to the main body of the church is through a narthex with a ceiling decorated with beautiful mosaic work in the most mesmerising blue and gold. Over its lifetime the church has been damaged several times, most recently in 2003 when the nearby British Consulate building was bombed. The present layout includes five aisles, making it larger than the original building. It has a glorious gold iconostasis, the Greek Orthodox style of altar consisting of finely carved flat wood panels and access doors for the priests and clergy, interspersed with pictures of saints, Jesus and Mary of course, lovingly gilded and painted in deep, bright colours. The church interior is a visual euphony is there's such a thing, only more than pleasing to the eye with myriad old gold coloured columns, elaborately decorated pulpits and highly polished wooden thrones and seats. Light bounces off every surface, mixing intoxicatingly with the smell of incense.

Address: Han Geçidi Çıkmazı No 6, Asmalı Mescit, Beyoğlu

After doing a bit of research I discovered there are two other entrances, one in Meşrutiyet Street and the other through Hazzopoulos Passage. The one on Istiklal Street is the easiest to find because the church tower is just visible from the main drag. Also, Han Geçidi Çıkmazı is very close to Sent Antuan Kilisesi, that's the Church of Saint Anthony of Padua. If you're already going there you can easily cross over to Meryem Ana. Even if it's not a Sunday and you can only enter the narthex you'll get a good idea of the different religious aesthetics.

Opening times: 08.30-16.00, 7 days a week. These times only refer to entry into the grounds and the narthex. The church itself is open on Sundays and on major Christian Orthodox holidays.

GLOSSARY

alem - metal crescent on top of mosque dome
ayazma - a holy spring
aziz - saint
bay - male, man
bayan – lady, wife
biberiye - rosemary
bimah – a desk on a raised platform in Ashkenazi
   synagogues where readings take place on
   the Sabbath
boiserie - ornate and intricately carved wood
   panelling used as interior decoration
cadde - road
camekan – also called a söyunmalık. Refers to space
   where people change before entering
   into the bathing areas of a hamam.
cami – mosque
cami avizesi – a mosque chandelier that takes the
   form of a large metal ring suspended
   from the main dome with lights
   attached to it
canim – my darling
catechumen – a person preparing for baptism into
the   Christian faith
darülfünun - a university
decal - design created on special paper that can be
   permanently transferred to another surface
   such as glass or porcelain
dede – a senior dervish
derviş - dervish
dolmuş – a shared minibus
durak – a passenger stop for buses and dolmuş
ebru – Turkish art of paper marbling

gelin - bride

hac – the Hajj is the pilgrimage all Muslims are expected to make to Mecca during the last month of the Islamic year at least once in their life if they can afford to do so. It's one of the Five Pillars of Islam.

hamam – Turkish bath

han – traveller and trader inns with accommodation and depots, found in urban settings

hararet - the heat chamber in a hamam

harem – the section of a house designated for women only, also known as a seraglio in a palace

iconostasis – large panelled wall decorated with icons in Orthodox churches that separates the nave where the congregation stands or sits, from the sanctuary, the area around the altar considered the holiest spot in the church

imam – religious leader of a Muslim community

imaret - soup kitchen attached to a mosque which provides free food for the needy

istasyon - station

iyi geziler – good trip/happy wandering

kadın – woman, female

kasır - a pavilion or summer palace

khedive - representative of the Ottoman Empire in Egypt

kıraathane – reading house, derived from Arabic

kırlıngıc – a traditional carpentry method in which beams are joined together by creating interlocking fan-tail shaped cut outs at

each end. Also known as a dovetail
technique.

koru - grove or small wood

köşk – a pavilion or summer house

kūfic - a type of handwritten Islamic script

lokum – Turkish delight

mastic – a chewy resin obtained from Mastic trees,
used in natural chewing gum, Turkish ice
cream and other food items

medrese – theological school usually located in the
grounds of a mosque complex

mevlit – Islamic memorial service involving
particular prayers read out at set times after
death

meydan – a city square

mihrab - the prayer niche in a mosque indicating the
qibla, the direction of the Kaaba in Mecca.
Muslims should face this way while
praying.

millet - folk or people, also a system used by the
Ottoman Empire to categorise the citizenry
by their religion for administrative purposes

mukarnas – also known as muquarnas, these
honeycomb shaped architectural devices
are built into half domes of mosques to
provide support and act as transition
points in the design

musalla - stone rests coffins are placed on in mosque
courtyards

narthex - the room connecting the outside world to
the church interior. In the past, people
doing penance for their sins or those
preparing for baptism or confirmation

were only allowed to enter this section of the church.

ocakbaşı lokantası - grill restaurants

Okey - game using tiles in which players compete to score the most points

Osmanlı - Ottoman

otobüs - bus

pazar - weekly local outdoor markets

pazarlık - bargaining

peron – platforms buses and trains depart from

polycandelon – lights suspended from a triangle composed of three chains, used in Orthodox churches

Rum – Turkish citizens of the Orthodox faith descended from the Byzantines of the Eastern Roman Empire. Also called Greek Turks.

revzen - coloured glass windows set into walls of mosques and tombs above eye level to let in light

salep - a flour made from a type of wild orchid root

şadırvan - the ablutions fountain where people wash before entering the mosque to perform their prayers

şalvar – baggy pants worn by men and women. The excess fabric is designed to accommodate the second coming of Mohammad so that when he is born again, he will be caught in the folds of the pants and not hit the ground.

sebil - a public fountain for the free distribution of water

şehzade – son of an Ottoman sultan

selamlık – portion of a house reserved for men

Selçuk - Seljuk

hasoda – privy chamber

sokak - street

sur - city walls of Istanbul

tabhane - a hospice, usually in the grounds of a mosque complex

tahmis - coffee roasting

tavla – backgammon

tragacanth – a type of natural white gum derived from the sap of a shrub of the same name that grows in parts of the Middle East

tramvay – tram line

tren - train

trompe l'oeil – style of painting that tricks the eye into perceiving scenes as being three dimensional

tuğra – sultan's signature

tünel - tunnel

türbe – tomb

tuvalet - toilet

vapur - ferry

vezir – vizier in English, a high ranking official in the Ottoman Empire

wagons-lits - French for train sleeper cars

wainscoting – wooden panelling that lines the lower part of the walls of a room

ABOUT THE AUTHOR

Lisa Morrow is a Sydney, Australia-born sociologist, travel article and essay writer who has lived in Istanbul and elsewhere in Turkey for almost 15 years. Although born to an activist mother who once chained herself to the gates of Parliament House in Sydney and a father who helped create advertisements that introduced fish fingers into every Australian home, Lisa had a fairly conventional upbringing. She grew up in a leafy middle class North Shore suburb, finished high school and then went to Sydney University. Once there she failed to find her niche and dropped out.

She then worked as a public service clerk, cleaner, sales assistant, waitress, bar maid and car counter, before going overseas. After landing in the UK Lisa hitchhiked to Ireland, backpacked in Europe and then arrived in Turkey just as the Gulf War was starting. While most tourists left as fast as they could, Lisa stayed on in the small central Anatolian village of Göreme for three months, a decision that was to change the course of her life. She spent the following years moving between Australia and Turkey, but made it back to uni and graduated with a BA Honours Degree in Sociology from Macquarie University. An academic career beckoned but the call from Turkey was louder. She now lives in Istanbul and calls Turkey home.

After working as a teacher of English as a second and foreign language for around a decade, Lisa made the transition to being a freelance writer. Her byline has appeared in CNN Travel, The New York Times, The Guardian, Aljazeera, BBC Travel, World Nomads, Fodors, Hyperallergic and elsewhere.

Lisa has written three essay collections, *Exploring Turkish Landscapes: Crossing Inner Boundaries* (2014), *Inside Out In Istanbul: Making Sense of the City* 2nd Edition (2015) and *Longing for Istanbul: The Words I Haven't Said Yet* (2021), as well as a memoir called *Istanbul Dreams: Waiting for the Tulips to Bloom* (2015).

She's also researched, written and recorded an audio walking tour of Kadıköy, on the Asian side of Istanbul. Listen as Lisa takes you step by step through her neighbourhood with *Stepping back through Chalcedon: Kadikoy Walk,* available through Voice Map.

Determined to scratch away the seemingly mundane surface of ordinary Turkish life to reveal the complexities of its rich and fascinating culture, there's no limit to Lisa's keen desire to dispel popular myths and misconceptions. This once led her to ask a butcher why sheep heads are displayed the wrong way up. Despite being lectured to by a man clearly convinced she thinks Turkish sheep are born with their heads on upside down, Lisa continues to look for answers to this and other Turkish cultural conundrums. To find out what she's up to at the moment, follow her on her website and social media accounts listed on the next page.

Inside Out In Istanbul website:
https://www.insideoutinistanbul.com/
Twitter personal:
https://twitter.com/goreme1990

IG Inside Out In Istanbul:
https://www.instagram.com/insideoutinistanbul/

FB Inside Out In Istanbul page:
https://www.facebook.com/InsideOutInIstanbul

FB Lisa Morrow Author page:
https://www.facebook.com/LisaMorrowAuthor

OTHER BOOKS BY THE AUTHOR

Exploring Turkish Landscapes: Crossing Inner Boundaries

The first time Lisa Morrow went to Turkey she was just one of many young people on the great pilgrimage to Europe and beyond. The colourful sights, sounds and smells of foreign countries appeal

EXPLORING
TURKISH
LANDSCAPES

CROSSING INNER
BOUNDARIES

LISA MORROW

to their need for adventure and excitement. When the enterprise becomes too trying, there is always the safety of a return ticket to fall back on. After a given period of time they're expected to return, a little older and a lot wiser. While some go for a year, others never make it back.

At first Lisa only travelled across the vast expanses of Turkey as a visitor, but then she began to stay for longer and longer periods of time. Her initial glimpses of a culture less western than eastern were replaced by an awareness that Turkey is at times both and yet something more. These experiences became a metaphor for an inner journey from the known to the unknown and back. The uncompromising nature of Turkish culture and society meant she had to accept what she saw

208

without changing it. In so doing she started to question who she was and look for an alternative way of being.

Inside Out In Istanbul: Making Sense of the City
2nd Edition

For most people, Istanbul is synonymous with its world-famous sights, the Haghia Sophia, the Blue Mosque and Dolmabahçe Palace. Yet a short ferry ride across the Sea of Marmara takes you from the beauty of the historical district of Sultanahmet to the shores of Asia, where a different Istanbul awaits. An Istanbul vibrantly alive with the sounds of roving vendors, wedding parties, street musicians and more. The stories in *Inside Out In Istanbul* take the reader beyond the tourist façades deep into this sometimes chaotic, often schizophrenic but always charming city.

INSIDE OUT
IN ISTANBUL

MAKING SENSE OF
THE CITY

LISA MORROW

Longing for Istanbul: The Words I Haven't Said Yet

From the moment Lisa Morrow first stepped onto Turkish soil in 1990, her love affair with the country has been tumultuous. She came to stay forever and then left for good many times, but could never get Turkey and more specifically Istanbul, out of her mind. The chaos, intensity and spirit of the city repeatedly called her back. It's a place where traditions clash with modernity and emotions overrule logic. In Istanbul Lisa's heart beats contentedly at being home and when she's away, whether in Turkey or elsewhere, she longs to return. Yet once there, a sense of longing remains. Istanbul's essence is elusive. It shimmers seductively just out of reach.

LONGING FOR ISTANBUL

THE WORDS I HAVEN'T SAID YET

LISA MORROW

In *Longing for Istanbul* Lisa writes about the passion, disillusionment, joy, despair and sheer determination that fuel her love for Istanbul. She tackles head on the events, attitudes and issues which mean life in Turkey isn't always plain sailing, while acknowledging she wouldn't choose to live anywhere else.

Istanbul Dreams: Waiting for the Tulips to Bloom

In 2010 Lisa Morrow moved to Istanbul with her husband Kim, permanently. Having already lived

in the city and Central Anatolia before, on top of
travelling extensively throughout the country, she was sure the transition would be simple. However while Turkish culture seems easy to understand, you only have to scratch away the surface and the complexities can be overwhelming.

When they arrived in Istanbul Lisa was still trying to overcome the effects of her mother's death and struggled to know who she was. Her feelings of uncertainty were exacerbated by dealings with Turkish real estate agents, bureaucracy and cultural differences, as well as friendships with Turks who seemed the same as her but were in fact very different. The stress of getting settled was only just starting to abate when she had to

ISTANBUL DREAMS

WAITING FOR THE TULIPS TO BLOOM

LISA MORROW

rush Kim to hospital and then received bad news from home.

When the dream of living in a foreign country is rudely shattered by gritty reality, you have two choices. Turn tail and run or bravely face what life throws at you. Welcome to a roller coaster ride through the unpredictability of life in Turkey.

Books in Turkish

Türkiye'yi Keşfederek Sınırlarımı Aşarken (Exploring Turkish Landscapes)

Lisa Morrow Türkiye'ye ilk geldiğinde Avrupa'ya ve başka diyarlara doğru muazzam bir sefere çıkan gençler kervanının bir üyesiydi. Yabancı ülkelerin manzaraları, sesleri, kokuları rengârenk gelir bu insanlara, serüven ve heyecan iştahlarını kabartır. Macera çok zahmetli hale geldiğindeyse, tek bir geri dönüş bileti yardımlarına koşuverir. Belli bir vakitten sonra biraz yaş almış, çokça olgunlaşmış halde eve dönmeleri beklenir. Bazıları bir yıllığına ayrılır, bazıları hiç dönmemek üzere.

Türkiye'nin pek çok yerini ilkin bir ziyaretçi olarak gezen Lisa, ülkede giderek daha uzun süre kalmaya başlar. Batıdan ziyade Doğuya daha yakın bu kültüre dair ilk izlenimlerinden sonra Türkiye'nin kimi zaman her ikisine eşit uzaklıkta, hatta Batılı veya Doğulu tanımlarının da ötesine geçen bir ülke olduğunu kavrayacaktır. Uzlaşıya pek mahal vermeyen Türk kültürü ve toplumu Lisa'yı gördüklerini değiştirmeden kabul etmek durumunda bırakır.

212

Böylelikle kim olduğunu sorgulamaya başlar ve varoluşuna alternatif aramaya koyulur.

Türkiye'yi Keşfederek Sınırlarımı Aşarken eserinde okur, Türk gelenekleri ve inançlarını kişisel bir derinlikle yorumlayarak kendini yeniden keşfeden bir kadının duygusal yolculuğuna eşlik eder.

INDEX

Mosques

Museums

Other churches

Parks & Groves

Pavilions & Summer Palaces

Printed in Great Britain
by Amazon

27706957R00126